New Trends in
Employment Practices

Recent Titles in Contributions in Labor Studies

New Trends in Employment Practices

AN INTERNATIONAL SURVEY

Walter Galenson

CONTRIBUTIONS IN LABOR STUDIES, NUMBER 34

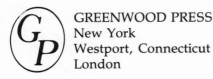

GREENWOOD PRESS
New York
Westport, Connecticut
London

Library of Congress Cataloging-in-Publication Data

Galenson, Walter.
    New trends in employment practices : an international survey /
Walter Galenson.
        p.   cm.—(Contributions in labor studies, ISSN 0886–8239 ;
no. 34)
    Includes bibliographical references and index.
    ISBN 0–313–27629–3
    1. Industrial relations. 2. Labor market. 3. Quality of work
life. I. Title. II. Series.
HD6971.G225   1991
331—dc20   90–45325

British Library Cataloguing in Publication Data is available.

Library of Congress Catalog Card Number: 90–45325
ISBN: 0–313–27629–3
ISSN: 0886–8239

First published in 1991

Greenwood Press, 88 Post Road West, Westport, CT 06881
An imprint of Greenwood Publishing Group, Inc.

Printed in the United States of America

The paper used in this book complies with the
Permanent Paper Standard issued by the National
Information Standards Organization (Z39.48–1984).

10 9 8 7 6 5 4 3 2 1

CONTENTS

PREFACE

The winds of change have been blowing through the labor markets of the industrialized nations. The velocity has varied from one country to another, but the direction is very much the same. International imitation may be part of the cause, but fundamental economic forces affecting all nations are largely responsible for the recent developments.

What are these forces? None is more important than the surge of women from the home to paid employment. Women's traditional role has given way to a labor market status that is rapidly approaching that of men. The reasons for this development are not entirely clear. On the one hand, opportunities may be widening in occupations that women find attractive. On the other hand, they may have been pushed into jobs to help their families take advantage of the increasing volume of available goods and services. Whatever the cause, there can be no doubt about the result: major changes in patterns of work designed to accommodate women.

A second factor is industrial restructuring. Manufacturing is no longer the dominant employer of labor. It has been surpassed—in some countries by wide margins—by industries that produce services rather than goods. A whole range of new skills has emerged, often under the impact of changing technology. The relative decline of blue-collar jobs has eroded the historical core of trade unionism. Programs have been mounted to preserve declining manufacturing industries in the belief that jobs, economic growth, and national security are at stake, but to little avail.

Less basic but nonetheless significant has been a shift in the objectives that motivate people to work. When the provision of daily bread was paramount, the quest for higher income had first priority. With greater affluence, other goals have emerged, among them the desire for more leisure, enhancement of job security, improvement in the quality of working life, and more adequate provision for post-retirement years.

Finally, within the past two decades, an intangible but increasingly significant employee demand has surfaced for what may be called industrial democracy. This is not a new idea. Many forms of employee participation in making business decisions have been advocated for at least a century, but attempts to put them into effect have not proved successful. What is new is the implementation of participatory schemes that are not only economically viable but may even lead to higher productivity.

The policy innovations that have emerged in response to these developments vary from one country to another. The precise responses depend in considerable measure on public attitudes toward government intervention in the labor market. Where this is more or less accepted, as in most European countries, the legislative route is often followed. Where the prevalent ideology opposes government interference, as in the United States and to a lesser extent Japan, the private sector is expected to provide the solutions.

The pages that follow are devoted to an exploration of the many experiments that have been tried during the past two decades in response to the new challenges. Promoting industrial democracy at the enterprise and plant levels, improving the quality of working life, preserving jobs and finding new ones when layoffs do occur, rearranging work schedules to accommodate the new entrants into the labor market, and programs to take into account the increased longevity of working life are among the topics covered.

The countries selected for comparative analysis are the major industrial nations of the democratic world—France, Germany, Great Britain, Japan, and the United States. Sweden has been added to this group because it is known for its imaginative programs affecting labor. A final chapter on Soviet labor practices is included because it illustrates the manner in which many of the same problems are handled in a Communist society. The Soviets have to deal with unemployment and with the tensions arising from the dual obligations of work and home, for in their labor force, women are more heavily represented than in any Western country. Recent events there illustrate graphically the strength of the demand for greater democracy at the enterprise as well as the political level. Adversarial relationships between management and labor appear to persist in a system in which the state is the only employer in spite of long-held Soviet dogma to the contrary.

New Trends in
Employment Practices

Chapter One

INDUSTRIAL DEMOCRACY AT THE ENTERPRISE LEVEL

The quest for industrial democracy goes back more than a century. It has many different roots: syndicalism, Catholic social doctrine, worker cooperation, Fabianism, and guild socialism among others. In the United States, liberal businessmen such as Edward Filene and Henry S. Dennison sponsored their own versions.

The goal was to provide employees with an avenue for influencing decisions of immediate relevance to their welfare both within the enterprise and in the wider economy. The organizational reforms that were proposed ranged from trade union control (syndicalism) to joint labor-management discussion groups. What they all had in common was a rejection of Marxism with its emphasis on government ownership and control of the basic means of production.

Some proponents of industrial democracy regarded employee participation in making business decisions a matter of social ethics. Pope John XXIII, building on similar pronouncements by earlier popes, included the following statement in a 1961 encyclical, entitled *Mater et Magistra*:

Like our predecessors, we are convinced of the legitimacy of the workers' ambition to take part in the life of the undertaking in which they are employed. We consider that workers must be given an active part to play in the management of the concern in which they are employed, whether the concern be public or private. Every effort must be made to make every undertaking a real human community which will make a deep impression on the relationships, the duties, and the work of each of the members.

Those who approached industrial democracy from a political point of view argued that while a democratic order of society provided employees with full civic rights, these rights were not extended to the work place, where they spent a good portion of their waking hours. Some went so far as to maintain that democracy in the work place was more important to workers' well-being than participation in general elections. Another line of argument emphasized the economic significance of enterprise-level democracy. Worker participation might enable employees to play a more creative role in the organization and prosecution of work, leading to greater efficiency and maximization of output. It is this approach that is the current favorite.

Employers have never been enamored of the idea of worker participation. They maintain that it is erroneous to draw parallels between the powers of government and private enterprises. The government can levy taxes and can use force to ensure compliance with its laws. Private managers, they argue, must be able to make quick decisions. Firms cannot be run efficiently if parliamentary-style debates are permitted. Moreover, an enterprise has no coercive power over its employees who can quit their jobs if they are dissatisfied.

Many trade unions have also opposed the concept of worker participation. In their view, collective bargaining is essentially an adversarial process in which unions must rely upon the unalloyed support of their members. If workers become too closely identified with enterprise problems, their militancy may be reduced. Employees are and should be concerned with the prosperity of the firm for which they work, but the interests of the two are not always compatible. Since it is difficult to secure a mutually agreeable division of income by consensus, employees must sometimes be prepared to inflict financial damage on the firm and its stockholders to further their own interests.

The economic efficiency argument has been challenged. Employers point to a lack of technical knowledge and business skills that would enable workers to make sound decisions. Their short-term concern with secure jobs and higher income may come into conflict with the long-run viability of the firm. For example, employees would generally oppose the closing of an unprofitable plant if their jobs were at stake. Hard decisions must be made by those with a broader view of the economic environment if the firm is to survive.

SYNDICALISM

The doctrine of syndicalism had its origin in France and spread to Italy and Spain. The early trade union movements in all three countries came under its influence, and some vestiges still remain, particularly in one of the major French trade unions, the Democratic Confederation of Labor. In Italy, Mussolini borrowed its terminology but perverted it to fit the Fascist labor structure. Syndicalism even found a temporary foothold in the United States in the pre–World War I Industrial Workers of the World (IWW).

The French word for trade union is *syndicat*. To syndicalists, the trade union should be the basic social, economic, and political unit. Therefore, the machinery of parliamentary democracy is rejected. Participation in political parties under capitalism meant acquiescence in a system dominated by the enemies of the working class. The class struggle should be carried on primarily by strikes, which would gradually erode capitalist power. All strikes, whether won or lost, were considered a form of revolutionary gymnastics designed to build worker militancy; sabotage was regarded as an auxiliary weapon. The eventual overthrow of capitalism would be accomplished by a general strike, bringing all activity to a halt and forcing capitalists to relinquish their property and power. The syndicalists, however, did not advocate armed revolt.

The traditional state would be replaced by trade union bodies. Each enterprise would elect a union committee, which would then establish regional committees and eventually a national union federation. The national organization would function as an overall coordinating mechanism, but the principal locus of power would remain in the local union of the enterprise. The syndicalists did not go into detail about the feasibility of running a complicated economy through so decentralized a system.

Syndicalists were strongly opposed to Communism. They feared that state ownership of industry would strengthen the central government and lead to greater oppression of working people. One of the first things that the Bolsheviks did when they gained power in Russia was to suppress the syndicalist movement. An interesting sidelight was the fate of William (Big Bill) Haywood, the redoubtable leader of the American IWW, who was indicted for criminal syndicalism in 1917. While out on bail, he left the United States and made his way to the Soviet Union, where he was not well received. He was allowed to live out his years in dingy quarters, but when he died, he was entombed in the Kremlin wall, the Communist pantheon. His end symbolized what happened to the syndicalist movement, which was crushed by the Communists once more during the Spanish Civil War.

PRODUCER COOPERATION

During the early years of capitalism, arduous working conditions led employees to seek an alternative mode of production that would afford greater independence. Instead of working for wages, working people were urged to pool their resources, establish workshops and factories, and share in the profits to the exclusion of capitalist intermediaries. This idea was very popular during the latter half of the nineteenth century and led to the formation of many such enterprises. These should not be confused with consumer cooperatives, which are concerned with the distribution of goods rather than their production.

For a number of reasons, few producer cooperatives were successful. The lack of sufficient capital was perhaps the greatest obstacle. Few cooperators were able to marshall adequate funds out of their own savings, and the banks were usually unwilling to finance them. The absence of managerial ability was another problem. It was the rare craftsman who both possessed sufficient business acumen and was willing to use it in the service of a cooperative. His preference was to set up his own shop. There was also a good deal of dishonesty among the cooperators themselves—it was not uncommon for the treasurer to abscond with the funds of the enterprise.

In his famous book, *A Theory of the Labor Movement*, Selig Perlman cited additional reasons for cooperative failures. Internal dissension was common. Workers felt that cooperation was almost as desirable as self-employment, until they learned by experience how unpleasant cooperators could be to one another. Cooperative workshops also tended to undersell private firms in order to secure a share of the market and in the process failed to provide adequate depreciation reserves. When they did become profitable, some cooperatives expanded production by hiring wage earners, thus diluting the cooperative structure. Perlman observed that the enterprise would eventually come under the control of one or two of the more able members who would buy the others out.

Cooperatives were disliked by private employers, who often did what they could to make life difficult for the cooperators. An account of what happened to the Union Mining Co. of Cannelburg, Indiana, illustrates this point:

After expending $20,000 in equipping the mines, purchasing land, laying tracks, cutting and sawing timber on the land, and mining $1,000 worth of coal, they were compelled to lie idle for nine months before the railroad company saw fit to connect their switch with the main track. When they were ready to ship their product, it was learned that their coal could be utilized for the manufacture of gas only, and that contracts for supply of such coal were let in July, nine months from the time of connecting their switch with the main track. In addition, the company was informed that it must supply itself with a switch-engine to do the switching of the cars from its mine to the main track, at an additional cost of $4,000. When this was accomplished, they had to enter "the market in competition with a bitter opponent who has been fighting them since the opening of the mine." Having exhausted their funds, and not seeing their way clear to securing additional funds, . . . they sold out.[1]

The cooperative movement was particularly strong in the United States. At the movement's peak in 1886, there were 135 known cooperative enterprises operating there, and more that had not been tabulated. One reason for the demise of the Knights of Labor, a national trade union that competed with the American Federation of Labor, was its close identification with the cooperatives, extending on occasions to financial assistance. When most of the cooperatives failed, the Knights went down with them. A similar fate befell the co-ops in other countries. A few of the early ones have survived in the British shoe and printing industries, but they never achieved a sufficiently large scale of production to make them significant factors.

The producer cooperative form of organization has reemerged recently, but under greatly different circumstances. Employees of failing companies in the United States have raised capital and taken them over rather than seeing their jobs disappear. These are a far cry from the nineteenth-century enterprises, for they are usually large in size and run by professional managers. One of the first was a meat-packing concern that was bankrupt; it survived briefly under employee ownership but could not operate profitably. A major steel company is still producing under cooperative auspices. The problem faced by these and other similarly placed concerns is that they begin on a precarious economic base. The plant and equipment that they inherit are often outmoded, which is one reason for the original private failure. Their markets may be shrinking, and they have to pay a high price for good managerial talent. There are successful cooperative enterprises in other countries, particularly the Mondragon group in Spain, but the outlook for producer cooperation as a means of promoting industrial democracy does not seem bright.

THE WEBBS

Sidney and Beatrice Webb were the first to develop the theory of collective bargaining and to put into modern perspective the roles of trade unions and management. They considered the small, independent workshop to be inimical to the interests of working people. They saw the vertical division of society into separate enterprises, in which the individual firm and its employees shared a common interest, as inferior to a horizontal division, in which workers looked upon themselves as members of the working class with interests opposed to those of the employing class. This formulation had a great deal of influence on the philosophy of trade unions, particularly in Britain, where the unions have been cool to the notion of close labor-management cooperation at the enterprise level.

The Webbs took a dim view of the wisdom of endowing trade unions with a share of managerial authority. To them, trade unions were no better qualified to determine what was to be produced than any other collection of individual citizens. Unions did not have the business and engineering expertise to judge what materials and equipment should be employed in the productive process. When it came to the conditions under which human agents were to be used in production, however, trade unions had a major role to play. For the Webbs, collective bargaining was the best approach to industrial democracy.

The Webbs were among the founders of the Fabian Society, whose doctrines helped provide the British labor movement with an antidote to the Marxist philosophy taking root in much of the rest of Europe. Founded in 1884, the society was named after the Roman general Fabius, who defeated Hannibal in the Second Punic War by using a cautious strategy of delay and avoidance of battle until the time was ripe for action. The Fabians were socialists in that they favored the gradual extension of state power over economic life, to be accomplished entirely by democratic means.

The Webbs were concerned about the administrative machinery of the state, particularly its efficiency. Working from the ground up, they did a good deal of research on the manner in which municipal governments operated, for which they were dubbed "sewer socialists" by contemptuous Marxists. The Fabians were ambiguous on the question of how far the state should go in the control of enterprise, but whatever the form of any future collective society, trade unions were to continue to be key players. Neither the Fabians nor the proponents of any other brand of socialism foresaw what has become a crucial problem in modern socialist states: whether trade unions have a useful function when government owns or controls enterprises, and if so, how to define the limits of their activities.

The idea of collective bargaining as the essence of industrial democracy is still very much alive, particularly in the United States. John T. Joyce, the president of the Bricklayers' Union and one of the more thoughtful of American trade union leaders, has recently written that "the process of collective bargaining is the departure point, because, indeed, it is the only base upon which we can build industrial democracy in the United States. For working people, furthermore, the process of collective bargaining is, and will remain, the core of industrial democracy."[2]

GUILD SOCIALISM

The founder and chief proponent of this movement, which had its heyday in Britain after World War I, was G.D.H. Cole. It has its origin in syndicalism, but adjusted for British realities. The fundamental idea was that, in order to free the wage earner from oppression, the wage system would have to be destroyed and the control of industry transferred to the modern guilds—the trade unions. The medieval guilds had been associations of craftsmen who attempted to maintain price and quality standards. Anyone who wanted to join a guild had first to serve an apprenticeship and then pass an examination to determine whether he had acquired the requisite skill. He then became a journeyman and for a time was employed by a master craftsman, although he hoped eventually to open his own shop.

Guild socialism rejected both syndicalism and full state socialism. The state would not control production, but it had to be preserved in order to protect consumers against possible abuse by producers.

Industry would be directed by the trade unions. Cole feared state power in a collective society, so one of the functions of the trade unions would be to serve as a check on the bureaucracy.

To fulfill their obligations, unions would have to undergo radical structural adjustments. Craft unions would be replaced by industrial ones that would have to operate entire industries. Local unions would be coterminous with individual shops or factories and would constitute the building blocks of a National Guild.

During the transition to full guild socialism, unions would assume joint control with owners of enterprises. Cole considered this a step forward rather than collaboration with the class enemy. He was ambivalent on the question of whether the nationalization of industry should precede the assumption of control by the unions, fearing that the state might then refuse to relinquish control and institute state socialism instead. He did concede, however, that some industries, notably the railroads and coal mines, would have to be nationalized at an early date.

Although it aroused a great deal of contemporary discussion, nothing much came of guild socialism. British trade unions continued to oppose any doctrine that preached collaboration with capitalists, although they did favor the nationalization of industry. Yet the ideas generated by Cole and his followers have influenced subsequent efforts to define a system to implement industrial democracy without risking the imposition of a degree of governmental power that would undermine the essential purpose of industrial democracy—to give employees at the shop level some control over the policies of the enterprises for which they work.

CODETERMINATION IN WEST GERMANY

Codetermination is easily the most important experiment in employee participation at the enterprise level in recent years and perhaps ever within the framework of a capitalist system. It has characterized German industrial relations for most of the period since World War II. Codetermination is embedded in the world's fourth-largest economy, which has been highly successful in terms of economic growth.

Germany was in ruins after the defeat of the Nazis in 1945. Anyone who visited the country's major cities after the cessation of hostilities would have predicted that it would take decades to restore a semblance of pre-1933 conditions. Indeed, for a few years, the economy operated largely on a barter basis. Unemployment was high, and a great many people were engaged in cleaning up rubble and making streets passable.

With the currency reform of June 1948, trade unions began to function once more after a hiatus of fifteen years. The German Trade Union Federation (DGB) was established in the fall of 1949. It grew rapidly. By 1950 it had 5.5 million members, a figure that has risen to 7.7 million at the present time. Several smaller labor federations are independent of the DGB: the Confederation of German Civil Servants (800,000 members); the German Salaried Employees Union (500,000 members); and the Christian Trade Union Federation (300,000 members).

The DGB was constructed along strict industrial lines. Each of its seventeen affiliated national unions represents employees in a major industry. The largest and most important of its national affiliates is the Union of Metal Industry Workers (IG Metall) with 2.5 million members, which represents employees in fifteen sub-industries, including automobiles, steel, machine tools, shipbuilding, aerospace, and electrical engineering. More than any other organization, IG Metall has shaped the system of codetermination.

Codetermination originated in the Ruhr steel industry in 1947. The leaders who helped form the new trade unions, some of whom had spent the war years in concentration camps, were determined to prevent any repetition of the financial support that the Ruhr steel barons had given Hitler. This so-called "special" codetermination was extended to coal mining in 1951. Under this plan, supervisory boards (akin to corporate boards of directors in other countries) are composed of equal numbers of members representing stockholders and employees, with a neutral chairman chosen jointly. The employee members typically represent various labor echelons; for example, if there were an eleven-member supervisory board, two of the five labor members might be the chairman of the works council and his deputy (the works council, an integral part of the system, is dealt with in the next chapter). Two additional members might be delegated by the national union, while the fifth might be nominated by the DGB.

Management functions are carried out by a three-member board, one of whom supervises industrial relations and personnel matters. This so-called labor manager cannot be appointed or dismissed without a majority vote of the labor members of the supervisory board.

It has been a consistent goal of the German trade unions to extend "special" codetermination to the rest of industry, but thus far they have not succeeded. The system now in effect is based on legislation, enacted in 1976, that amended a previous law. In firms that regularly employ more than 2,000 workers, supervisory boards are composed of an equal number of employee- and stockholder-appointed members, while in smaller firms (500 to 2,000 employees), the employees designate only one-third of the board members.

At first glance, the arrangement for the larger companies might seem like parity for the employees, but this is not the case. The reason is that senior executives and salaried employees are entitled to board representation in proportion to their numbers, and their representatives can be expected to vote with the stockholder members. Moreover, in the event of a tie vote, the board chairman, who is elected by the stockholder members, casts the deciding vote. In the final analysis, the employees can be outvoted by the stockholders, which is not the case under "special" codetermination.

The largest enterprises, those with at least 20,000 regular employees, would normally have a supervisory board of twenty. Ten are elected at a meeting of stockholders. Of the other ten, one is a salaried employee, one a manager, while the rest are elected by either wage earners or their delegates. At least five of the latter are normally employed in the enterprise; this group usually includes the chairman of the works council and his deputy. The remaining three members can be nominated by the trade unions and need not be employees.

The management board is appointed by the supervisory board, with a two-thirds majority required. If this majority is not forthcoming, a mediation committee consisting of the supervisory board chairman, the vice-chairman (usually an employee representative), and one additional representative from each side is given the task of finding a solution. It submits nominations to the full board, which at this stage can make the appointments by a simple majority vote with the chairman casting the deciding vote in the event of a tie. On this crucial matter of selecting top management, the employee representatives are thus in a minority position.

The management board includes a labor director, but he need not have the approval of the employee board members, who can neither veto his appointment nor cause his dismissal. This differs from the situation under "special" codetermination. However, it would be unusual for an individual who did not have the confidence of the employees to be selected for this post.

According to a recent estimate, about 7.7 million of the 23 million employees in Germany are represented on supervisory boards, while the rest are either government employees (who have consultative rights only), employees of non-profit organizations, or employees of smaller enterprises that are not covered by the Codetermination Act but that nevertheless may have instituted some form of representation. All the major German companies are included in the mandatory representation group.[3]

A question that immediately arises concerns the appropriate role in collective bargaining of labor members of the supervisory board. Several of them have been nominated by national unions or by the DGB itself. Does this mean that the union simultaneously represents the employer and employees? The interests of the two may be different: for example, the firm may need to cut wages in order to maintain its competitive position while workers may feel that they deserve a wage increase. British and American unions have raised this question, among others, in opposing codetermination.

The nature of the German collective bargaining system has helped to mitigate this problem. Most bargaining takes place on a national or regional level between national unions and associations of employers. Collective arguments tend to be multi-employer in scope. German trade unions do not have local unions that engage in bargaining. The majority of agreements are interpreted and administered at the enterprise level by works councils that have no organic connection with the unions. Thus, what might be a prolific source of conflict, were collective bargaining carried out at the enterprise level, is less likely to occur under the arrangements that are in effect.

But this is not the entire story. About one-third of all collective agreements cover only a single enterprise. Moreover, individual firms have a voice in determining the terms offered by their associations, so that there is still room for conflict. This might have been the case in 1984, when IG Metall staged an eight-week strike involving 350,000 workers in an effort to gain a 35-hour week with no reduction in pay in order to reduce unemployment. The union won a 38 1/2-hour week; the cost to the automobile companies was $75 million a day in lost production.

This was an unusual event, however. Codetermination can work only if decisions are taken after thorough board discussion of the issues and careful analysis of the relevant data. In practice, it appears that stockholder board members rarely use their majority to force policies on the labor minority but seek rather to achieve consensus by compromise. This does not mean that employers greeted the introduction of the present system of codetermination with any enthusiasm. In fact, they reacted to the 1976 act by a court challenge to its constitutionality, but were rebuffed by the Federal Constitutional Court in 1979. Some employers have attempted to evade the requirements of the law by splitting their companies into smaller units, but by now most employers have accepted the necessity of complying with the requirements of codetermination and do so with good grace.

As for the unions, they still seek complete parity of representation, but their chances of winning it hinge upon the accession to political power of a majority Social Democratic government. Even in that event, it is by no means certain that the Socialists would be prepared to force the issue in the face of what is likely to be bitter employer opposition. Moreover, it is not clear that full parity along the lines of the coal and steel system would be more than a symbolic gain for the unions.

The best way to secure an understanding of how the formal structure of codetermination is translated into practice is to look at situations in which there were serious labor and management differences of opinion. Fortunately, there is an excellent study available of how Volkswagen, the big automobile manufacturer, handled some major problems. The findings will be summarized briefly, but the interested reader is urged to secure a copy of the full report.[4]

In the early 1970s, Volkswagen faced a serious financial problem because of declining sales in its principal foreign market, the United States. Management considered it necessary to reduce the company's labor force by 18,500, or 17 percent. At that time, before the enactment of the 1976 law, there were twenty-one members on the supervisory board, of whom fourteen represented the stockholders (including four representatives of the federal and state governments, which were major stockholders); the other seven represented labor. All of the latter were either IG Metall officials or works council chairmen of major plants.

The managing director of the company, Herman Leiding, had become increasingly alienated from the plant works councils. It was felt that more flexible leadership was essential if the reductions in force were to be achieved. He was forced out and replaced by Toni Schmucker, the top manager of a large steel company in which he had been operating under "special" codetermination and had gained the confidence of IG Metall.

The first proposal toward staff reduction was a plan for closing a plant that produced the NSU car and employed 11,500 workers. This idea was vigorously opposed by the union and dropped. A second scheme called for a staff reduction of 25,000 over a two-year period, to be accomplished by normal turnover and early retirement; only if these measures proved insufficient could there be a maximum of 10,000 dismissals. Prior to the formal submission of this plan to the supervisory board, the union developed an alternative providing for attrition of 20,000 with a top limit of 4,700 dismissals. After a long discussion, the board adopted the management proposal by a vote of fourteen to seven, the labor members all voting in the negative. There is evidence that the latter recognized the need for the larger force reduction but opposed it for tactical reasons. The upshot was that despite growing unemployment, many more employees than expected took their severance pay and resigned. An increase in car sales made further dismissals unnecessary. What this episode demonstrates is that the company was able to react to economic necessities with sufficient speed and that the union was prepared to cooperate because it was fully informed of the company's financial needs.

It is interesting to compare this event with what sometimes happens under similar circumstances in the United States, where management typically makes redundancy decisions without consulting the employees or their representatives. For example, on May 24, 1985, Art Berens, president of a local of the United Automobile Workers at the Donaldson Company in St. Paul, Minn., a manufacturer of auto parts, was asked to meet with the company negotiators to discuss a new contract. When he arrived, he was informed that the plant was to be closed immediately. At the same time, this announcement was being read to the employees, some of whom had been with the company for as long as twenty-seven years. Similarly, on March 29, 1988, the first shift workers at a canning facility of the Pabst Blue Ribbon Co. in Tampa, Florida, who were all members of the Steelworkers Union, were notified that the plant was to be closed; the workers were given forty-five minutes to leave the property. Later shifts learned of the closing from the news media.[5]

The operation of codetermination in Germany may be illustrated by the way that Volkswagen handled another type of decision. Declining sales in the United States in 1974 led the management to recommend the opening of a plant there in order to be closer to the market and to be independent of currency fluctuations. The union agreed that it was essential to defend the U.S. market but was concerned about the potential loss of German jobs. The company developed a plan that involved closing a plant at Emden, among other things. Under pressure from the union and before formal submission of the plan to the supervisory board, the management agreed that the U.S. plant would only assemble vehicles from parts to be manufactured in Germany. It was also agreed that the U.S.-assembled cars would not be exported to Europe and that the closing at Emden would be avoided by moving work there from other plants.

The Volkswagen cases illustrate how codetermination functions. Any major management initiatives that may affect the personnel are discussed informally with employee board representatives prior to formal consideration by the entire board. Every effort is made to secure tacit or open employee agreement before the board votes. Management can put its policies into effect even if it is impossible to achieve consensus, but this does not occur frequently.

The system is not without its costs. In response to the question of whether the original management proposal to open a plant in the United States would have been more profitable than the one finally adopted, Schmucker, the managing director of Volkswagen, replied:

> It is beyond doubt that it would of course have been less expensive to produce everything in the United States. This is, however, not a matter of paying a tribute to the union but rather one of common insight that with the gradual approach two things can be realized. First, we reduce our financial commitment and with it our risk. And secondly, we minimize the risk to employment which in the last weeks and months has understandably been very much in the minds of our workers.[6]

A general evaluation of the efficiency of German codetermination will be postponed until the next chapter, where the second major structural element in the system, the works council, is considered. Suffice it to note here that codetermination in Germany is now forty years old and has been shaped by a process of trial and error. It is the longest lasting of the modern social experiments designed to permit employee participation in the enterprises where they work. It seems to be firmly established, with little likelihood of reversion to the more usual situation in which managers make decisions and employees simply accept them.

BOARD REPRESENTATION IN OTHER
COUNTRIES

Germany was the pioneer in codetermination, but a number of other countries have adopted variants of the scheme, including the Scandinavian countries, Austria, and the Netherlands. In 1972, the Swedish Trade Union Federation gave up its opposition to board representation and sponsored legislation requiring that in all companies with more than 100 employees, unions were to have the right to appoint two members to the corporate boards. The minimum was reduced to twenty-five employees in 1976, when the law also stipulated that a union-appointed director had to be included in the executive committee of the board.

Denmark adopted similar legislation in 1974. Companies with more than fifty workers were required to have two union representatives on their boards. In Austria, employee representation on corporate boards was set at one-third of the total membership, with the employee members to be elected by the works councils of the enterprises. A somewhat weaker representation right prevails in the Netherlands, where the board itself can co-opt employee members, subject to the veto right of the shareholders.

Perhaps the strongest form of codetermination outside Germany is to be found in Norway. In firms with at least fifty employees, employees have the right to elect one-third of the members of the board of directors. Where there are more than 200 employees, another body, called the corporate assembly, must be established if the employees so desire. The assembly consists of at least twelve members, one-third elected by the employees and the rest by the shareholders. In turn, the assembly elects the board of directors. The assembly has access to all books and records; it is the final authority in investment decisions of any substantial size and in any projected operating changes that may involve the reallocation of the labor force. It may also determine the maximum amount of dividend distributions. The assembly is typically larger than the board of directors, and its purpose is to bring decision-making authority closer to the shop floor.

The work of analyzing the long experience with these systems remains to be done. In light of the lack of serious management protest and the fact that their continuance has not become a political issue, the implication may be drawn that both employers and employees have learned to live with them. Leftist groups have complained that labor directors are too far removed from the worker, while employers sometimes express concern about the amount of time required to make decisions. As in Germany, however, codetermination plans appear to have become a permanent feature of the industrial relations environment.

A Royal Commission under the chairmanship of Lord Bullock held hearings in 1977 on the possibility of introducing codetermination in Britain. The commission heard concerns expressed by both management and union witnesses. Among these were the fear that union power would be undermined; that it would be difficult for unions to divide their energies between board representation and collective bargaining on behalf of workers; that worker representatives are bound to have split loyalties; that labor directors might reveal confidential information to the detriment of the enterprise; that investor confidence might be undermined, making it difficult to raise capital; and that labor and capital might conspire to raise profits and wages at the expense of the consumer.

After examining these and other arguments, the commission came out squarely for codetermination. It expressed the conviction that it was the best way to utilize the energies and skills of the working population:

to provide greater satisfaction in the workplace and to assist in raising the level of productivity in British industry—and with it the living standards of the nation—is not by recrimination or exhortation but by putting the relationship between capital and labor on a new basis which will involve not just management but the whole workforce in sharing responsibility for the success and profitability of the enterprise. Such a change in the industrial outlook will only come about, however, as a result of giving the representatives of the employees a real, and not a sham or token, share in making the strategic decisions about the future of the enterprise which in the past have been reserved to management and the representatives of the shareholders.[7]

The Commission recommended legislation whereby unions in companies with more than 2,000 employees could name directors equal in number to those elected by shareholders, if a majority of the union members favored such action. The two sides would then jointly name neutral members. This proposal was strongly opposed by the business community and by a number of trade unions. It was never implemented.

American management overwhelmingly opposes codetermination, as do most American unions, although some unions might favor it as a means of augmenting their dwindling bargaining power. There have been isolated instances of unions gaining board membership, but this has generally taken place when the companies were in dire financial straits and needed union support and concessions in order to remain in business. The best known case is that of the Chrysler Corporation, which was seeking a government subsidy in order to avoid bankruptcy. Western Airlines similarly conceded employee board representation, profit sharing, and stock ownership to its four major unions in return for a package of wage and work-rule concessions. But in the absence of crisis situations, it will take a strong commitment on the part of union leadership, plus "highly unionized bargaining relationships where the union is secure and the employer sees no pragmatic alternative to accepting, working with, and enhancing the role of the union," to bring about movement toward board representation for the employees of American corporations. It cannot be said that these conditions are even on the horizon at the present time.[8]

EMPLOYEE STOCK OWNERSHIP

The notion that employees should become corporate stockholders and thus share in their company's prosperity became very popular in the United States in the 1920s, which is sometimes called the decade of welfare capitalism. Presumably employees' interests would thus be identified more closely with the success of the enterprise and they would make a greater contribution by improving their performance; it was never envisioned that employees would eventually accumulate enough stock to enable them to elect representatives to boards of directors. Quite a few employees did invest, and, as long as the stock market was booming, the plan gained adherents. With the market crash of 1929, many employee-stockholders lost their savings, and the popularity of the scheme came to an abrupt end.

The idea gained currency again in Europe after World War II, but this time with a more radical purpose behind it. It became a scheme for pooling employee stock ownership so that eventually the employees as a group could become sufficiently large stockholders to gain at least partial control over corporate policy. Trade unions in Germany, France, and Holland took up the idea, but it came to fruition in Sweden.

The Swedish plan was largely the work of Rudolf Meidner, then chief economist of the Swedish Federation of Labor. Its basic orientation can be judged from the following statement of its purposes:

1. [to] complement the policy of wage solidarity in such a way that the owners of highly profitable firms would not be enriched;

2. [to] counteract the growing concentration of capital, and hence the power, which is the concomitant of self-financing in a highly industrial economy; and

3. [to] reinforce wage earners' influence at the workplace through participation in ownership.

The proposal came at a propitious time for Swedish socialists. The welfare state was fully in place. The government's share of the national income was so great, the level of taxation so high, and the coverage of welfare programs so complete as to preclude further progress along traditional lines. Government ownership of industry did not appeal to the trade unions, with the Soviet model so close. The Meidner plan offered the possibility of a new approach to industrial democracy.

Employers strongly opposed the plan from the start, calling it "socialism by the back door." The plan contributed to the Social Democratic Party losses at the polls in 1976 and 1979. Nevertheless, the party continued to advocate it under trade union pressure and put it into effect after winning parliamentary elections in 1982. When the proposal was being debated in the parliament the following year, Swedish business interests organized a demonstration against its adoption. An estimated 100,000 people participated, a very large number given the auspices. The government nonetheless went ahead.

The legislation established five regional funds to be financed from two sources: a 20 percent tax on the net profit of firms in excess of specified levels and an increase of 0.2 percent in the employers' payroll contribution to the state pension system. The funds were to be invested in the stock of Swedish corporations, with each fund limited to a maximum of 8 percent of the voting shares of any single firm. This meant that the funds together could accumulate up to a 40 percent interest in a corporation—not a majority, but still effective control unless the remaining shareholders voted as a bloc. The funds were to pay dividends of 3 percent a year to the state pension system. Each fund was to be administered by a nine-member board of directors, at least five of whom were to represent the employees, so that the various union federations would have a potential majority if they voted together. Employer organizations were entitled to nominate members but refused to do so.

This scheme has a number of advantages from the union point of view. Since individual employees do not hold the stock in their own names, there is little danger of a loss of union solidarity. Employees presumably would not be deterred from striking against a firm in which they have no personal investments that might be jeopardized. The labor movement as a whole gains economic power and makes it less likely that corporations will adopt anti-union policies.

The fears of employers have not yet been realized. It is estimated that by 1990, the five funds together will own only about 5 percent of the total number of listed company shares. Some of the largest firms in the country have not paid profit taxes to the funds because of their financial situations. Moreover, even in Sweden, what constitutes profits is subject to creative accounting. The funds have thus far been financed primarily by the relatively small payroll tax.

What will happen in 1990 when the scheme is to be reviewed by the parliament is difficult to forecast. Ardent socialists may want to lift the 8 percent ownership restriction. Employers will undoubtedly press for the abolition of the funds. The trade unions may be in a quandary: if the funds are permitted eventually to acquire majority positions in corporations, the union-dominated boards of directors of the funds would be responsible for corporate policy; they might not want to combine that function with their collective bargaining role.

It is too soon to assess the impact of the funds on the Swedish economy. One thing seems clear, however: the scheme is not likely to further cooperative relationships between employers and employees. Whether it will have any effect on productivity is questionable. When the Danish trade unions were considering a similar plan (they have not had the votes to have it enacted into law), they tried to bring the funds closer to the employees by maintaining separate accounts for each individual that could be withdrawn upon retirement and by permitting the employees of a company to vote that company's shares held by the fund.

An American plan reminiscent of those in the 1920s came into vogue in the 1970s. The Employee Stock Ownership Plan (ESOP) was given considerable impetus by the enactment of the Employee Retirement Income Security Act of 1974, which permits a corporation to deposit its stock in a trust fund for the eventual benefit of its employees. Such contributions may constitute a corporate tax deduction of up to 15 percent per annum of the compensation earned by the plan's beneficiaries. An amendment in 1984 introduced an additional tax incentive; it provided that banks that lent money to retirement funds to enable them to buy the stock could deduct half the interest received from such loans from their gross income. For example, a bank that earned interest from an ESOP loan at a 10 percent rate would pay taxes on only 5 percent.

Stock accumulated by an ESOP is credited to the accounts of individual employees in proportion to their compensation. Distributions must begin within a year of retirement, disability, or death. Should an employee resign or be discharged, the distribution must begin not later than the fifth year after such event. In the great majority of plans, the stock is voted by the ESOP trustees rather than by the employees for whom it is being held. However, the trustees are required to solicit the view of the employees and to vote the shares according to their instructions.

It has been estimated that in 1986 there were about 8,000 employee plans in existence. Most were stock bonus plans, which are less restrictive than ESOPs. For example, there is no requirement to invest primarily in the stock of the corporate employer, and holdings may be diversified. ESOPs proper covered only 690,000 employees in 1985.[9]

The proponents of the ESOP concept cite three main goals: to improve the economic performance of the sponsoring organization, to spread stock ownership among a larger number of people (their slogan is "every man a capitalist"), and to provide funds for capital formation. The evidence on the first is mixed: Some who have looked into the matter claim that employee stock ownership raises productivity, while others are skeptical. There is no convincing evidence that ESOPs have motivated employees to work more effectively. For one thing, the rewards for heightened effort are too remote, nor is the extent of ownership sufficient to provide a real sense of participation. In a large enterprise, an ESOP would typically own a very small proportion of total corporate stock.

ESOPs do broaden stock ownership. The U.S. General Accounting Office found that the average percentage of employees participating in ESOPs was far greater than the percentage of U.S. families owning stock. Most of the employee-stockholders would probably not own stock were it not for ESOPs. But overall stock ownership is very concentrated in any event; 41 percent of all publicly traded stock was owned by the 0.5 percent of families in the highest income bracket in 1983.[10]

As for investment resources, bank loans to ESOPs enable them to purchase corporate stock, with these loans to be paid off out of the future earnings of the corporations. Moreover, the tax advantage to the lending institution enables the corporation in effect to borrow money at a concessional rate of interest. The magnitude of ESOP adoptions is not yet sufficiently large to make them a significant source of investment funds.

Trade union attitudes toward ESOPs are mixed, depending on their experience. The Machinists' Union made wage and other concessions to Eastern Airlines in return for stock ownership, only to have the company taken over by a strongly anti-union employer and eventually go into bankruptcy. Other unions see ESOPs as a possible entering wedge into corporate decision-making. There have been cases in which ESOPs actually acquired companies, but usually where there were financial difficulties. In 1984, the 8,500 employees of Weirton Steel bought the company and have continued to operate it after taking substantial wage cuts. Other efforts of a similar nature have not proved successful; a good example is Rath Meat Packing, which failed after several years of employee ownership.

Although both the Swedish and American plans involve vesting employees, directly or indirectly, with stock in their employers, their purposes are quite different. The Swedes hope to achieve greater equality of wealth and enhanced social control over private enterprises. Individual employees benefit only in the sense that the stock funds contribute to their government pension system. ESOPs do add more to the benefit of employees by directly raising their pensions, but there is no broader social purpose. The Swedish stock funds are designed to further socialism, while American ESOPs are intended to strengthen capitalism. Neither can be said to make a significant contribution to industrial democracy, at least as perceived at the level of the shop floor. It is there that we now turn.

NOTES

1. John R. Commons et al., *History of Labor in the United States*, Vol. II (New York: Macmillan, 1946), p. 437.

2. John T. Joyce, "Expanding Economic Democracy," *An Issue Paper from Social Democrats USA*, 1988, mimeographed.

3. Volker R. Berghan and Detlev Karsten, *Industrial Relations in West Germany* (Hamburg: Berg, 1987), p. 130.

4. Wolfgang Streeck, *Industrial Relations in West Germany* (New York: St. Martin's Press, 1984).

5. These examples are from the *AFL-CIO News*, May 14, 1988.

6. Quoted in Streeck, *Industrial Relations in West Germany*, p. 102.

7. *Report of the Committee of Inquiry on Industrial Democracy*, chaired by Lord Bullock, Her Majesty's Stationery Office, January 1977, p. 160.

8. These issues are discussed in Thomas Kochan, Harry Katz, and Robert B. McKersie, *The Transformation of American Industrial Relations* (New York: Basic Books, 1986), pp. 178–205.

9. Bureau of National Affairs, *Employee Stock Ownership Plans* (Washington: Bureau of National Affairs, 1987), pp. 7–8.

10. U.S. General Accounting Office, *Employee Stock Ownership Plans* (Washington: GPO), February 17, 1986, pp. 32–39.

Chapter Two

INDUSTRIAL DEMOCRACY AT THE SHOP FLOOR LEVEL

Almost every European country has some form of employee organization other than a trade union at the plant or shop level. In some cases, they include only employees, while others are joint in that management representatives are also members. The functions of these bodies, which are known variously as works councils, enterprise committees, factory councils, or shop steward committees, vary widely depending, among other things, on legislation, trade union structure, and collective bargaining practices.

It is difficult to generalize about the importance of these councils, not only because of international differences, but also because of variation among firms within the same country. Some are powerful bodies that participate in a wide range of managerial decision-making. Others are limited to ensuring clean rest rooms, good food in the company cafeteria, and adequate recreational facilities. This chapter deals primarily with the councils that play a significant role in industrial relations.

GERMANY

The German works councils are an integral part of the codetermination system; as such, their constitution and authority are prescribed by law. Their importance is heightened by the fact that the national trade unions in Germany do not generally have local unions as part of their structures. Therefore, many of the functions performed by locals in other countries devolve upon the works councils. However, they are not completely independent, but are linked to the unions informally.

The basic legal document governing works councils is the Works Constitution Act of 1972, which provides that councils may be elected in all enterprises with five or more employees. Establishment is not automatic; either the employees or a trade union must take the initiative. It has been estimated that only about 19 percent of eligible firms have works councils, although these include 65 percent of all private sector employees.[1] The number of members is stipulated by law, ranging from one person in firms with fewer than twenty employees to thirty-one in firms with 7,000 to 9,000 employees, plus two more members for each additional 3,000 employees. Blue-collar and white-collar employees are entitled to separate representation in proportion to their relative strength.

All employees over eighteen years of age are entitled to participate in council elections, which are held every three years. Only employees of the firm may be members, unlike the supervisory boards on which outside trade union officials and experts may serve. Lists of candidates may be proposed by trade unions or by non-union groups of employees, with the winners elected from lists on the basis of proportional representation. About 80 percent of the winning candidates are members of unions affiliated with the DGB; IG Metall has been particularly effective in electing its members to the councils. This means that the unions are not excluded from workshop influence despite their lack of local organization.

Works council members enjoy special privileges. They may not be discharged while holding office or for one year thereafter. Their pay cannot be reduced below that of employees in comparable positions. They are entitled to time off without loss of pay while performing council duties, and the council chairman in large firms often devotes full time to council business. A new council member is entitled to three weeks of paid leave to attend a training course set up by state governments with the cooperation of unions and employer associations.

Works councils may not call strikes. Differences with management that cannot be reconciled through negotiation are submitted to a tripartite arbitration board for final adjudication. Union representatives may attend works council meetings as advisers, and councilors can engage in union activities within the plant, further strengthening the union position. Moreover, works councils are forbidden to deal with conditions of employment normally determined by employer-union collective agreements.

Apart from these restrictions, works councils enjoy a broad range of authority that is often embodied in plant agreements. The degree of authority varies depending upon the nature of the issues involved. So-called "social" issues require works council agreement before management may act on them; that is, the works council has the full right to codetermination. Among these issues are the following, all specified by statute:

1. Commencement and termination of working hours, including breaks.
2. Temporary reduction or extension of hours worked.
3. Time, place, and form of payments for work.
4. Scheduling and administration of leaves.
5. Use of technical devices to monitor employee performance.
6. Health and safety measures.
7. Form, structure, and administration of company social services.
8. Remuneration arrangements, including piece and bonus rates, but not wage levels.

The authority of the works councils is not as great when it comes to the organization of work, but it is still substantial. This purview includes scaling down or closing a plant or department, mergers, significant changes in plant organization or equipment, and the introduction of new methods of work or production techniques. In these matters, management must consult with the works council before taking action and must negotiate a plan that protects the interests of the labor force. If no agreement can be reached, mediation by a government official may be invoked, but in the end the employer may still implement the changes. In that event, however, a "social plan" is required, compensating employees for any economic loss that they may suffer, including the possibility of lump-sum payments.

On personnel matters, the works council in larger plants can require management to establish general criteria for hiring, discharge, and transfer. Before management actually takes any personnel actions, the works council must be consulted, though its consent is not necessary. If the council believes that the employer is violating the plant agreement or a law, however, it can bring the case before a special labor court for resolution.

Employers are required to meet with their works councils at least once a month, and they apparently do so. The councils in turn are supposed to report to an assembly of all workers in the plant every three months, on company time, but this is not always done. The assembly can take a position on works council decisions, but such action is not binding. The employer may attend the assembly meeting and address it. That this body is not of great importance is evidenced by the fact that on average only about 25 percent of the employees attend, despite the fact that they lose no income if they do.

Although white-collar workers are entitled to proportional representation on works councils, they are in fact generally under-represented. Why this is so is a matter of speculation; it may be due to the same factors that account for their lower rate of unionization—a greater sense of individualism and closer identification with management. Women are also under-represented; even when they constitute a majority of the employees, they are often a minority among council members.

The chairman of the council, who is elected by its members, can play a very important role in the plant, often spending full time on council duties. There is no limit on the number of three-year terms he or other councilors may serve. Reelection is common, so that long-term councilors learn a great deal about company operations. They appear to be generally satisfied with their influence on "social" issues, but less so when it comes to personnel matters. Many have complained that they are not given sufficient information on recruitment, although their participation in dismissal decisions appears to be adequate.

It will be recalled that one or more works councilors serve on corporate boards of directors. In this capacity, they have a voice in the appointment of the members of the managing board, including the labor manager. This gives them access to whatever corporate information they do not receive as works councilors. But they do have a problem of dual relationships. On the one hand, they may take a narrower policy view than the trade unions, which are more concerned with the workers in the industry as a whole rather than in a single company. On the other hand, workers may come to perceive them as too remote, particularly those who serve for long terms, or as too close to management. Indeed, if a council is to be effective, it must establish rapport with management, often developing personal friendships.

A survey was recently undertaken to determine how effective German workers thought the various representative bodies were in protecting their interests. The works councils ranked first, followed by unions, supervisory board members, and labor managers.[2] But the distinctions are basically not clearcut. "The dilemma of the works councilors and of the other employee representatives is that they are elected by the workforce but their chances of becoming nominated and elected depend on the support of the trade union. In fact, the same people who exert the participatory rights have gradually taken over managerial responsibilities."[3]

The trade unions have been concerned about maintaining their power in the face of works council popularity. It has even been suggested that the big IG Metall strike of 1984 was designed to remind the membership that unions are vital to their interests. There is some feeling that workers might be better served by strong local unions instead of works councils. IG Metall began to tackle this problem as early as the 1950s by providing for shop stewards at the plant level. Unlike the works councilors, they are union officials and subject to its discipline. Their job is to help recruit new members, collect dues, and nominate candidates for the works councils. By the mid-1970s, IG Metall had one steward for every twenty members in the metal-working industry. But the strategy of reducing works council influence did not prove successful. The difficulty was that works councils are part of the codetermination structure and shop stewards are not. Works councils take care of local matters, while collective bargaining is mainly a national union affair. In occasional controversies between works councils and shop steward committees led by radicals, the former have won out.

From the employer point of view, the largest influence of works councils appears to be in the greater importance accorded to manpower planning. The labor manager has at least as much status as those concerned with production, sales, and finance. Employers also face the necessity of preparing decisions carefully because they may have to be defended before the works councils. This places an additional burden on management, but it makes it more likely that managerial decisions will be accepted by the employees with good grace.

Volkswagen may be cited as an example of a works council in operation.[4] At its Wolfsburg plant in 1978, the works council had sixty-three members, of whom twelve represented white-collar workers. Participation in the election of these councilors was high—85 percent of those eligible to vote. IG Metall candidates won forty of the blue-collar seats, the rest going to an affiliate of the Christian Federation, a small competitor of the DGB. IG Metall also won eight of the twelve white-collar seats.

By law, Volkswagen was required to release a minimum of thirty-eight councilors from their normal duties for full- or part-time council work. By local agreement, the company voluntarily released all the councilors and paid them a foreman's salary plus ten hours of overtime, giving them earnings 50 percent higher than average plant earnings. Every councilor was provided with an office and typing assistance.

The law stipulated that central councils were to be set up in multi-plant companies, and this was done at Volkswagen. The central council included the chairman of all the plant councils plus additional delegates. Domiciled at Wolfsburg, its task was to take up difficult questions referred to it by the individual plant councils. There were also 800 shop stewards elected for three-year terms by union members, but their status was clearly subordinate to that of the works councilors.

The central council maintained close contact with the national headquarters of IG Metall, which provided it with legal and economic advice. The chairman of the national union was a member of the supervisory board of the company, while the chairman of the central council was a member of IG Metall's national executive committee, facilitating coordination of policy between the two organizations.

Observers differ in their assessments of the extent to which codetermination as a whole confers decision-making authority on employees and unions. A recent study reached the conclusion that "codetermination grants the trade unions and the mostly unionized members of the works councils extensive rights of information, but only limited rights of participation. These rights do not entail substantial limits on management authority. It is also clear that codetermination promotes the integration of workers and that it has contributed to social peace."[5] Another analyst reaches a more positive conclusion on the impact of the system: "Gradually the unions have developed an infrastructure matching their claim for codetermination and enabling them to deal with the employers on many more issues than traditionally defined by the scope of collective bargaining. The relative success of codetermination was possible only because the employers and the managers became convinced that such a system provided an efficient way of managing the employment relationship."[6]

What seems to be true is that the precise limits of codetermination vary from company to company. There are firms in which neither the works councils nor the labor board members have much input into managerial decisions. At the same time, the well-documented Volkswagen case suggests that under some circumstances worker participation in Germany has gone well beyond the level prevailing in most Western nations. Many American and European trade unions would give a great deal to have comparable legislation on the statute books of their countries.

It is not possible to assess with any degree of precision the impact of codetermination on the performance of the German economy. There are too many variables involved to single out the separate effect of codetermination. On the negative side, Berghan and Karsten have cited the loss of manpower flexibility because of the difficulty of securing works council approval of dismissals, in effect closing the internal labor markets of large firms.[7] It may be noted parenthetically that the same effect is often found in American firms as a consequence of seniority clauses in trade union contracts.

On the other hand, improved employee morale because of greater job security and a sense of participation may have enhanced productivity, but the available data cannot be used to substantiate this claim. One of the problems is that there was a substantial slowdown in the rate of growth of the German economy during the 1980s. This has been attributed variously to appreciation of its currency, excessive subsidization of agriculture, and high taxes. This brought about a weak growth in labor productivity, but codetermination is not cited as a contributing cause.

By one labor index, codetermination does appear to have had a positive effect. Apart from the 1984 strike in the metal trades, to which reference was made above, Germany appears to have enjoyed a degree of industrial peace during the past several decades matched only by that of Japan, whose labor unions cannot be compared with those of Germany in terms either of economic or political power. The irritants that are often behind work stoppages appear to be mitigated by the preliminary discussions at both corporate and workshop levels mandated by the codetermination system.

FRANCE

Unlike Germany, where the structure of plant-level representation is simple, France has a complicated network of local units. One layer has been superimposed upon another over the years, but the end result falls far short of German codetermination. French employers have been more reluctant than the Germans to deal with trade unions. Faced with three major competing labor federations, two of which are committed to the replacement of capitalism with some form of collectivism, there is an ideological barrier to the establishment of close employer-employee relationships. Three-quarters of the larger French enterprises are affiliated with the National Council of French Employers (CNPF). Collective bargaining is carried on mainly at the industry level; plant-level bargaining is regarded by management as a risk to its authority. For their part, the unions fear that bargaining and cooperation at the plant level will result in even greater divided allegiance among the workers and will reduce their militancy.

The oldest of the plant-level groups consists of the employee delegates, whose existence was mandated by Popular Front legislation in 1936. They are elected annually by proportional representation from lists of candidates proposed by the various unions, with technicians and supervisors voting separately. The number of delegates varies with the size of the firm. Their authority is limited to the presentation of individual and collective grievances.

Next, legislation requiring the establishment of works committees in firms employing fifty or more persons was enacted in 1946. Election to the committees is based largely on trade unions' lists of candidates, with a two-year term of office. One of the best ways of judging relative trade union influence is by the results of works committee elections, since paid union membership is low. In 1982, the Communist *Confédération Générale du Travail* (CGT) won almost one-third of the votes, the quasi-syndicalist *Confédération Française Démocratique du Travail* (CFDT) gained 23 percent, while the Social Democratic *Force Òuvrière* (FO) received about 12 percent. Almost 20 percent of the votes went to nonunion candidates. In addition to the elected members, each union with sufficient membership may send one observer to committee meetings.

The main function of the works committee is to promote employer-employee cooperation. It cannot negotiate basic employment conditions or present grievances. Though primarily a consultative body, it is entitled to a considerable amount of information. The employer must furnish it with quarterly reports on production, finance, and employment. More detailed annual reports cover profitability and investments; these may be examined by outside consultants employed by the committee. Plans for new projects and mergers must be discussed in advance with the committee.

Works committees do have the right of codetermination over some employee welfare programs, including profit-sharing arrangements and plant canteens and libraries. They must approve the appointment or dismissal of the plant medical officer. In larger enterprises, they establish sub-committees dealing with health, safety, and training. On work rules, they have only consultative rights; in financial and economic matters, they are restricted to the receipt of information.

A third echelon of representation was the direct result of the general strike of 1968. Unions gained the legal right to set up local plant sections to arrange for the collection of dues and to distribute union information through specified numbers of shop stewards. The sections have authority to bargain, and they apparently do so on an informal basis. "Trade unions are able to claim the credit for any improvement in pay and conditions without compromising their longer term objectives by signing agreements that might be thought to be supporting the status quo. For their part, employers are able to maintain an impression of making decisions unilaterally."[8]

A fourth level of plant representation was introduced in 1982 when a Socialist government enacted legislation that gave employees the right of "collective expression" on matters relating to labor conditions. The proponents believed that despite the existence of three shop-level bodies, employees did not have adequate means of communicating their concerns to the employer. Under this arrangement, firms with more than 200 employees are required, in cooperation with the unions, to meet with groups of employees who can express their views directly to the employer without the intermediation of unions or works committees.

These groups are not negotiating bodies. They are designed rather to stimulate discussion of matters of mutual interest. Employers opposed the legislation, fearing that the right of unions to help determine the agenda of the discussion would expand union power. The reaction of the unions was interesting: FO opposed the scheme on the grounds that employees can present their views better through elected representatives; CFDT had been campaigning for freer individual expression and welcomed the change; and CGT apparently believed that the new forum would merely provide an additional means of waging class warfare. The 1982 law consolidated previously separate committees on health, safety, and the improvement of working conditions and allowed for calling in outside experts at the expense of the employer. It also permitted employees who felt that their working conditions were too dangerous to stop work.

A survey of the 2,400 employee "expression" agreements entered into in 1983 revealed that a majority of them stipulated between three and six meeting hours a year; they generally allowed supervisors to play a leading role in the discussions. Most unions had been willing to enter into such agreements.[9] An article on the various pieces of relevant legislation, including that of 1982, reached the following conclusion about their chances of improving shop-level relationships:

Another obstacle may lie in the proliferation of levels and procedures for negotiation and consultation. . . . This problem can only be avoided if the functions of each level of negotiation are clearly defined and accepted. . . . [T]he new legislation poses more questions than it answers. The government's aim is undoubtedly to persuade the various parties to come to an agreement in the hope of bringing about consultation and better understanding. If this strategy succeeds, the development of new practices will completely reform the industrial relations system of France. But it also carries the risk that the system will remain unchanged and that the new institutions will be diverted from their original aims and used as new resources in maintaining the traditional system as it is.[10]

Movement toward industrial democracy in France appears to be blocked by the strength of the existing labor market institutions, which, unlike those of Germany, were not shattered by the years of war and occupation. Management remains strongly averse to any voluntary concession of authority to employees or their representatives. The division of the labor force into three major federations contributes to its inability to impose some form of codetermination on employers, even if that were the goal. Intense competition among the unions makes it difficult for any single organization to appear too cooperative with employers, lest it lose votes in works committee elections and fall in status. The anti-capitalist ideology of the Communist-controlled CGT further limits any plan designed to increase the profitability and productivity of individual firms at the potential cost of working-class solidarity. Even the German trade unions have shown concern with what has been called company-egoism, and the French unions are much more vulnerable, given their traditions.

What the French experience demonstrates is that merely legislating the creation of employee representation plans is not sufficient to endow employees with participatory authority. If the labor market parties are not committed to cooperative relationships, the new units become merely additional forums for the settlement of disputes. This is not to say that employee delegates, works councils, and the like are not useful. They reduce open conflict and help stabilize the industrial relations system. But by themselves they have not taken France very far on the road to industrial democracy.

SWEDEN

Codetermination in Sweden operates through local trade union organizations rather than through independent works councils. The basic legislation governing the present system is the 1976 Act on Codetermination at Work, which contains the following provisions, among others:

1. The employer must negotiate with the local union or unions representing his employees before effectuating any important changes at the workplace, including such matters as switching to a new line of business, reorganizing production methods, or selling the firm. Changes affecting individual workers, such as personnel transfers, also fall within this obligation.

2. If agreement cannot be reached on the proposed changes, the local union may refer the matter to its national union. In that event, the implementation of the changes must be deferred until negotiations are concluded at both levels. If there is an emergency, such as concern for plant safety or important public interests, the employer may act prior to the conclusion of negotiations, although the negotiations must continue. Avoiding damage to property or situations in which it is obvious that the employer must act quickly also exempt him from the duty to negotiate first. It is important to note, however, that where the parties cannot reach agreement on the issue involved, the employer is free to make a unilateral decision. The union has the power to delay action but not to prevent it.

3. The employees have the same right to information about the enterprise as the employer himself. This includes financial, production, and personnel data. The union is entitled to examine the corporate books and may employ outside experts for this purpose. However,

this right does not extend to private matters unrelated to the business, to tactical matters involved in a labor dispute, or to particularly secret or confidential matters, although the employer is enjoined from interpreting the latter exceptions too broadly. A union representatives in possession of confidential information may not reveal it to anyone except the union's executive committee.

4. In the event of a dispute over any working conditions except compensation, including such matters as overtime or work assignments, the union's interpretation of the relevant collective agreement provisions takes priority, and it is the employer who must appeal to the grievance machinery. On wage matters, the employer must immediately institute negotiations and file for resolution of the controversy with special labor courts if agreement cannot be reached. The interesting thing about this provision is that it reverses the almost universal practice of the employer acting first and the union filing a grievance.

5. The employer must negotiate with the union before subcontracting any work. If subcontracting appears to involve a breach of law or contract, or if it is contrary to accepted practice in the industry, the union may veto it. The purpose of this provision is to prevent the transfer of work to subcontractors who disregard current pay schedules or violate safety regulations.

This legislation was quickly implemented in the public sector, where procedural agreements were reached between the unions, the management of state enterprises, and the State Bargaining Office, which represents the government in collective bargaining for 400,000 state employees. Things moved more slowly in the private sector because of negative employer attitudes toward the legislation. It was not until 1982 that agreement was reached between the employers' federation and the two major unions representing the blue-collar and white-collar employees respectively.

This Agreement on Efficiency and Participation, stressing the need for greater productivity and profitability, was in fact addressed as much to the economic situation in which Sweden found itself as to the legislative mandate. Swedish consumer prices rose by almost 22 percent between 1980 and 1982, compared with 12 percent for Germany and 17 percent for the United States. Sweden's gross domestic product increased by only 1 percent during 1982, and its international competitive position, as measured by unit labor costs and the export value of manufactured goods, was deteriorating.

The agreement encourages the introduction of new technology, although the unions are entitled to consultation before implementation. The agreement also provides that employee consultants, paid for by the employer, are to be given access to all corporate records that might be necessary to evaluate financial and production experience. An arbitration board has been established to interpret the agreement in the event of any dispute that cannot be resolved through direct discussion between the parties. Joint labor-management councils are to be set up on the enterprise level to promote the purposes of the agreement.

It is too soon to determine what effect the legislation and the subsequent agreement will have on Swedish industrial relations.[11] Employer concerns that their managerial authority would be sharply curtailed have not been realized. Conversely, the expectations of the legislation's more radical proponents that the scheme would lead to greater social control of industry have not materialized. Management is required to negotiate on a wider range of issues than had previously been the case, but it still retains the right to make the final decisions. Consultation absorbs a fair amount of management time, but some managers believe that the negotiation procedures have improved the quality of decisions.

The question of whether the codetermination scheme has substantially increased shop-floor employee participation remains unresolved. It is true that employee representatives receive a great deal of information and now have a basis for reaching informed conclusions on an employer's situation and prospects. It would not be possible, for example, for a firm to negotiate a merger or takeover, or to close a plant, without full preliminary discussions with the employee representatives. This is still not codetermination on the German level, however. Those in the trade unions and the Social Democratic Party who believe that labor should have full equality with management in the formulation of business decisions may be expected to press for further measures.

One point can be made: Codetermination aroused much less employer heat than did the employee stock funds described in the preceding chapter. Employers are unlikely to attempt to overturn the codetermination system as it now operates. The scheme does represent a moderate change in the balance of managerial authority—employers in other countries might not be willing to characterize it as moderate—but the long tradition of labor–management cooperation in Sweden has made it relatively easy to fit the new arrangements into the prevailing system of industrial relations.

There are plenty of jeremiads on the subject of labor relations in Sweden. A pamphlet published by the Federation of Swedish Industries had this to say about the combined effects of the participatory legislation:

the existing laws on codetermination along with the proposal on collective funds provide sufficient conditions for a total socialization of the private sector within the Swedish mixed economy. . . . People realize that the hopes which the labor movement attaches to the co-ownership of companies cannot be achieved in the forms they have presented without seriously harming the efficiency of the economy.[12]

The labor movement rejects criticism of this nature. As far as it is concerned, employee participation can only help the economy by energizing the labor force to achieve higher levels of productivity. Thus far the argument is a stand-off. The economy remains mixed with private employers still in charge, while there is no evidence of greater employee motivation.

Sweden has been called a social laboratory for the Western world. Its recent experiments in industrial relations may either open a useful path for other nations to follow or turn out to be disastrous. In either event, it should be rewarding to follow the course of Swedish development in the years to come.

JAPAN

In order to explain the Japanese system of workshop consultation, it is necessary first to say something about the structure of Japanese trade unionism. On paper, Japanese unions appear to follow the Western model. Until 1989, there were two major labor federations in Japan, but on November 21, 1989, they were united in the new Japanese Trade Union Confederation (Rengo). A rival but much smaller federation (Zenroren) was inaugurated on the same day; it is critical of Rengo's "rightist line of labor-management cooperation."

Affiliated with Rengo are seventy-four national industrial unions with approximately 8 million members. These in turn are composed of enterprise unions, each one coterminous with a single firm. Where there are corporations with more than one factory or establishment, the enterprise unions are subdivided into branches with a fair degree of autonomy. In general, the structure of the enterprise union corresponds to that of the firm.

What makes Japanese unionism unique is that the locus of power is at the enterprise union level. This differs from the situation in other industrial nations, where power is concentrated either at the federal level or in the national unions. The Japanese labor federation is essentially a lobbying organization that represents the interests of its members before the national government and supports left-wing political parties. In this it does not differ from the labor federations of many other countries. The national unions, however, are quite different from their foreign counterparts. They do not engage in collective bargaining in the Western sense, nor do they have much control over their enterprise union affiliates. They do attempt to coordinate the bargaining activities of these affiliates, but they cannot formulate policies that are binding on them. In most countries, local unions are chartered or created by the national unions and are subject to central discipline. By contrast, Japanese enterprise unions are essentially autonomous; they can follow or reject national union recommendations depending on what they perceive to be the interests of their individual firms. This is company-egoism with a vengeance.

The key to understanding consultation at the workshop level in Japan is the apparent conviction on the part of both employees and their unions that there is a fundamental identity of interest between employees and the corporate employer. Whereas workers in other countries tend to identify either with the "working class" or with fellow craftsmen, Japanese workers identify with their employers. This identification stems in part from the prevalent system of tenured employment, which will be described in Chapter 4. As a Japanese scholar has put it:

Japanese unionists are really hesitant to cause any severe damage to the enterprise to which they belong. This is not because of their submissiveness to their employer or to management, but because of their identification with, or a sense of belonging to the enterprise to which they belong. If a worker serves a particular enterprise for many years during which he has good prospects for improving his wages, fringe benefits, skills, position, and status, it is quite understandable that he would acquire an interest in and concern about the enterprise; thus both employer and employee come to share a common desire to maintain the enterprise and to keep it prospering as much as possible. The enterprise becomes a kind of community to which employees tend to commit themselves.[13]

The result is that enterprise unions are reluctant to adopt an adversarial stance toward management. Apart from annual one-day demonstrations, strikes are virtually unknown. Other forms of non-cooperation, such as slowdowns, are never practiced. This gives rise to the question of whether the unions are in fact dominated by management. Union officials are often drawn from the ranks of supervisors, many of whom look forward to future management positions. Few professional union officers expect to make a career in the labor movement. A Japanese critic of the enterprise unions has observed that "trade unions are integrated into the organization of the enterprises from the bottom up and do very little in fulfilling their primary functions of acting as a check on management actions and exerting some control over working conditions, whereas the enterprises practice various systems of workforce management to intensify the workers' enterprise consciousness."[14]

Japanese enterprise unions are entrusted with the dual functions of bargaining on behalf of their members for wages and other conditions and of engaging in consultation with management at the workshop level. There are no works councils separate from the unions. An effort is made to keep the two processes separate; in a sense, consultation is a stage preliminary to bargaining.

There are two types of joint consultation. One takes place at the top corporate level. Management and union officials meet several times a year to hear reports on company progress and to discuss future plans. Any large-scale investment that is planned will be on the agenda, as will other matters that might affect the personnel. The second type involves so-called production committees that meet monthly to discuss planned production schedules. Some firms also organize workshop meetings that are attended by all the employees.

A compilation of the issues taken up in joint consultation reveals that prospective changes in job content, working hours and holidays, health and safety measures, and welfare benefits are presented in over 80 percent of establishments. Less common topics are recruitment and placement, rationalization, and training and education. Basic management policies were taken up in 63 percent of the enterprises surveyed. According to the records, in 79 percent of the meetings on this subject, the union representatives merely received an explanation; in 7 percent, their opinions were listened to; in 10 percent, there was discussion; and in 4 percent, some agreement was reached. In commenting on these data, a Japanese scholar has concluded that "joint consultation has supplanted collective bargaining as the most fundamental communication channel between management and labor."[15]

The basic role of employee participants in the various consultation bodies is to receive information and to make such suggestions as they see fit. They have no power to make decisions. Employees have no representatives on boards of directors; they can neither delay nor veto management policies. In theory, the enterprise union handles grievances, but even where grievance machinery is provided for by collective agreement, it is rarely used. Differences are said to be adjusted entirely through informal discussion, though there are no data on their outcome. Final arbitration by a neutral party is not the Japanese way of settling labor disputes.

Japanese experts point out that Japan is not unique in denying employees any right of codetermination, either at the top or at the workshop level. Neither trade unions nor employees in the United States, for example, enjoy such rights. But there is a crucial difference between Japan and the United States in this respect: Local unions in the latter country are backed by strong national unions and can exert considerable pressure, including work stoppages, on the whole range of matters included in collective agreements. Japanese enterprise unions, by contrast, are dependent on their own resources and are not inclined to rock the boat by confronting their employers in any event.

Assessing workshop consultation in Japan from the perspective of industrial democracy is like describing a glass as half full or half empty. Japanese scholars are almost unanimous in asserting that employees enjoy a large measure of control over their working conditions through constant discussion of policies and problems with management, all on an informal basis without any legal support. They stress collegiality and view the relationship between employees and management as "friendly and respectful rather than formal and contentious."[16]

Some outsiders view the Japanese labor scene differently. An official of the AFL-CIO, writing in a journal published by that organization, had this to say:

the argument that Japanese organization is more participatory than its American counterpart is ludicrous. In an article published in 1980 in the respected *sectai* magazine, Japanese reporter Satoshi Kamata made a number of startling revelations about the Japanese world of work. . . . In addition to describing the large number of suicides, industrial accidents, occupational diseases, production line speedups, and pressures at the workplace, Kamata had this to say about the conveyor-like Toyota management system: "It is no other than absolutism, which subordinates all the moves of goods and people, both within and outside the plants, to Toyota's will."[17]

Whether through choice or compulsion, Japanese employees work longer hours than their counterparts in other countries. A recent survey of the machinery and metal industries in Japan and Germany disclosed that annual working hours for a Japanese worker totaled 2,387, compared with 1,651 in Germany. Japanese workers took an average of six holidays a year, while German workers took thirty days.[18] Nor do Japanese workers' living standards accord with the nation's level of economic development. The Organization for Economic Cooperation and Development (OECD) estimated that the Japanese gross domestic product per capita in 1987 was 97 percent of that of Germany (based on purchasing power parities), yet Japanese worker housing standards were not only substantially below those of Germany, but also more expensive. A Japanese metal worker paid 7.3 times his annual wage for his home as against 4.3 years of wages for the German worker.[19]

The level of Japanese satisfaction with housing is reportedly very low. An article dealing with the housing conditions of Japanese workers contained the statement that the worsening housing problem "spurred many labor union leaders' awareness that problems relating to workers' lives may be left untouched as long as Japanese labor unions are only engaged in activities with firms."[20]

The Japanese argue that their population density makes the provision of housing a particularly difficult problem. There is truth in this argument, but countries with equal density have managed to house their people well; Holland is a good example. It is primarily a question of investment priorities; the Japanese government has steered investment toward industry and its accompanying infrastructures to the neglect of housing. Japanese housing and other living conditions might well have been more satisfactory to its working people if Japanese employers had faced powerful and aggressive trade unions like those of Germany.

Whatever criticisms can be leveled against it, the Japanese system of employee representation and consultation has given the country a remarkable degree of labor peace. It has been thirty years since any major Japanese firm has been shut down by a strike of any duration. Firms in the large-scale manufacturing industries can count on fulfilling their work schedules uninterrupted by labor controversy. This is undoubtedly an important factor in the remarkable performance of Japanese industry. It would have been even more remarkable had this been achieved under a regimen of industrial democracy. Despite the claims of the Japanese, this has not been the case. If some degree of employee participation in the formulation of managerial decisions is regarded as an important social objective, Japan is not an appropriate model for other countries to follow.

GREAT BRITAIN

Although a pioneer in the theory of joint consultation and participation, Great Britain has not advanced as far as its continental neighbors in practice. One of the main reasons has been the fear on the part of its long-established trade unions that close collaboration with employers would dilute the willingness of their members to press for higher wages and better conditions of labor. "Them and us" has been an important ideological concept in the history of the British labor movement, and it still persists to a considerable extent.

A Cabinet committee set up during World War I under the chairmanship of J. H. Whitley recommended the formation of joint labor-management councils at the national, industry, and local levels to improve the climate of industrial relations. Many of these so-called Whitley councils were set up, primarily in small-scale industry and in the public sector. Neither employers nor unions were enamored of them, however. By the onset of the Great Depression, most had disappeared.

Joint production committees were created during World War II to help meet military requirements. This experience induced some unions to advocate joint control of industry. In 1944, the Trades Union Congress (TUC) took the position that union officials should be appointed to the boards of directors of nationalized industries, but with the important proviso that they would then have to give up their union offices.

The concept of joint consultation through works councils was also accepted, but this policy never took hold. What happened instead was the proliferation of shop stewards as the principal representatives of employees at the workshop level. Among the reasons for this development were the weakness of the local trade union structure, the existence of multi-unionism (which complicated collective bargaining), and the preference of employers to deal with their own employees rather than with union field representatives who were often difficult to reach. In larger plants, the shop stewards, who were often quite independent of the unions, formed committees that in effect became the most important representation bodies.

Most of these committees were informal in that there was no provision for them in legislation or in collective agreements. They dealt with employers on a wide range of issues, including piece rates, pay structures, working rules, safety problems, and working hours. The committees were usually consulted before layoffs were effected. They also handled grievances. The Confederation of British Industries, the main employers' association, advised its members to provide shop stewards with a wide range of information in the interest of better relations, including data on profits, dividends, executive compensation, future plans, and manpower requirements.

At first glance, it appears that the shop steward committees are the equivalent of the German works councils, but in fact there are significant differences between the two institutions. The shop steward committees do not have the right of codetermination on any issues. What they get from employers in the way of concessions or information depends on what they are able to extract through their economic power. This can be considerable, since unlike the German works councils, they can call strikes to further their demands. Indeed, these short, unofficial strikes—unofficial in that they are not sanctioned by the trade unions—have been the bane of British industrial relations. Whatever influence the committees have on general business policy, as distinct from immediate conditions of labor, depends on employer attitudes and the experience and ability of the shop stewards themselves. Too often, shop stewards have been left-wing activists who sought these unpaid and sometimes arduous jobs in order to advance their political agendas—hardly a recipe for productive consultation.[21]

During the 1970s, when many British firms found themselves in economic difficulty and unions became concerned with chronic high unemployment, interest in joint consultation revived. Some company councils were set up with full-time union officials as members, and many companies began to provide their employees with more detailed information about current problems and future prospects. The TUC eventually came around to the idea that employees should be represented on corporate boards through their trade unions, with employees selecting half the board members, a proposal that was given short shrift by employers. But the TUC remains opposed to works councils on the German model; the idea that workers should be represented by non-union committees is not in line with British traditions. There appears to be little prospect of European-style codetermination finding its way to Britain in the foreseeable future.

THE UNITED STATES

Both management and unions in the United States have traditionally opposed employee participation through works councils. Where employees are organized, they are usually represented by local unions that have considerable authority to bargain on their own. American trade unions tend to be stronger and better financed at the local level than are unions in most countries of Europe. If there is to be any consulting or participation outside the bargaining nexus, the unions want to do it.

There have been some joint labor-management committees at the industry level and, as has already been noted, there are examples of union representation on corporate boards. There have also been a few beginnings of plant consultation apart from normal collective bargaining. At the General Motors' factory that produces the Fiero automobile, a network of committees oversees plant operations, with a union official on each one. At the top of the structure is an administrative group that includes the plant manager, senior staff, and the chairman of the union bargaining committee. The group receives a great deal of information on production and future plans, so that the union is kept well informed. Still, basic business decisions are made at a corporate level, above the individual plant, where the union is not represented.

A conference on the existing limited participation in the United States concluded that "worker participation apparently does help make alternative compensation plans like profit sharing, gain sharing, and ESOPs work better—and also has beneficial effects of its own. . . . Which forms of participation raise productivity the most?

We do not know. But giving labor a seat on the board of directors may be the least effective form of employee participation. Beyond that, there is controversy—and insufficient statistical evidence to resolve the dispute."[22]

American employers are extremely reluctant to yield any of their authority to make decisions unilaterally. A recent survey of participation developments concluded that "even if these experiments were to develop at a healthy pace, the American labor movement would still face severe problems in spreading this new approach to bargaining relationships where it lacks the power to gain or sustain a meaningful role in strategic managerial decision making. Sustained diffusion and institutionalization may therefore require the active support of public policy."[23] Such public policy support is not even on the horizon.

NOTES

1. Andrei S. Markovitz, *The Politics of West German Trade Unions* (Cambridge, U.K.: Cambridge University Press, 1986), p. 48.

2. U.S. Department of Labor, *Monthly Labor Review* (February 1986), p. 46.

3. Volker R. Berghan and Detlev Karsten, *Industrial Relations in West Germany* (Hamburg: Berg, 1987), p. 133–134.

4. This section on Volkswagen is based on Wolfgang Streeck, *Industrial Relations in West Germany* (New York: St. Martin's Press, 1984), pp. 49–53.

5. Otto Jacobi, "World Economic Changes and Industrial Relations in the Federal Republic of Germany." In *Industrial Relations in a Decade of Economic Change* (Madison, Wisc.: Industrial Relations Research Association, 1985), p. 233.

6. Friedrich Fuerstenberg, "Industrial Relations in the Federal Republic of Germany." In Greg J. Bamber and Russell D. Lansbury, *International and Comparative Industrial Relations* (London: George Allen & Unwin, 1987), p. 178.

7. Berghan and Karsten, *Industrial Relations in West Germany*, p. 136.

8. Keith Sisson, *The Management of Collective Bargaining* (Oxford: Basil Blackwell, 1987), p. 40.

9. Janine Goetschy and Jacques Rogot, "French Industrial Relations." In Bamber and Lansbury, *International and Comparative Industrial Relations*, p. 159.

10. François Eyraud and Robert Tchobanian, "The Auroux Reforms and Company Level Industrial Relations in France," *British Journal of Industrial Relations* 23 (July 1985), p. 256.

11. For a brief summary of varying opinions on the act, see Gus Cochran, *A Decade of Joint Regulation of Working Life in Sweden* (Stockholm: *Swedish Information Service*, Bulletin No. 34), December 1987.

12. Per Martin Meyerson, *The Welfare State in Crisis: the Case of Sweden* (Stockholm: Federation of Swedish Industries, 1982), pp. 59, 63.

13. Taishiro Shirai, "A Theory of Enterprise Unionism." In Taishiro Shirai, ed., *Contemporary Industrial Relations in Japan* (Madison: University of Wisconsin Press, 1983), pp. 137–138.

14. Shigeyoshi Tokunaga, "A Marxist Interpretation of Japanese Industrial Relations," in Shirai, *Contemporary Industrial Relations in Japan*, p. 324.

15. Takeshi Inagami, *Japanese Workplace Industrial Relations* (Tokyo: Japan Institute of Labor, 1988), p. 25.

16. Shirai, *Contemporary Industrial Relations in Japan*, p. 375. For a more elaborate development of this theme, see Takeshi Inagami, *Labor-Management Communication at the Workshop Level* (Tokyo: Japan Institute of Labor, 1983).

17. James N. Ellenberger, "Japanese Management: Myth or Magic," *American Federationist* (April-June 1982), pp. 8–9.

18. The Japan Institute of Labor, *Japan Labor Bulletin* (November 1988), pp. 2–3.

19. The Japan Institute of Labor, *Japan Labor Bulletin* (October 1988), p. 7.

20. Ibid.

21. For a good discussion of the role of shop stewards, see Hugh Clegg, *The Changing System of Industrial Relations in Great Britain* (Oxford: Basil Blackwell, 1979), pp. 41–61; David Farnham and John Pimlott, *Understanding Industrial Relations* (London: Cassell, 1983), pp. 354–390.

22. Allen S. Blinder, "Pay, Participation, and Productivity," *Brookings Review* (Winter, 1989/90), p. 38.

23. Thomas A. Kochan, Harry C. Katz, and Robert B. McKersie, *The Transformation of American Industrial Relations* (New York, Basic Books, 1986), p. 204.

Chapter Three

THE QUALITY OF WORKING
LIFE (QWL)

The quality of working life (QWL) is an amorphous term embracing
a number of concepts and activities. Among them are quality circles,
labor-management participation teams, humanization of work, job
restructuring, and the enhancement of employee creativity. Sometimes
the term includes employee participation in making managerial decisions, along the lines described in Chapter 2; it is often difficult to
distinguish between the two in practice. But the fundamental purpose of
QWL programs is *not* to enlarge the managerial authority of employees.
Although such programs may be seen as an effort to democratize the
shop floor, they differ in intent from the traditional meaning of industrial
democracy.

QWL programs have two basic goals: to raise productive efficiency
and to improve the physical and mental conditions under which people
work. The two goals are related in the sense that better working
conditions may raise productivity, but this does not always happen.
The emphasis differs among countries and among enterprises. Quality
circles, for example, are designed primarily to raise productivity, while
safety and health measures may be directed toward improving the
working environment, even at the expense of output.

QWL originated in the 1950s in American job enrichment theories
and in concepts developed by the British Tavistock Institute. These
related to a socio-technical system that included job structure, human
motivation, and technology. QWL received impetus from experiments
conducted at the Norwegian Work Research Institute and from the
Japanese adoption of quality circles in their expanding industries.
American management, particularly in the automobile industry, was

impressed with the Japanese approach, which was primarily aimed at raising productivity. Sweden, by contrast, became the pioneer of the more socially-minded Norwegian ideas, although productivity was by no means forgotten.

It is of interest that the advancement of QWL came primarily from management. Trade unions have been suspicious of, if not hostile to QWL, for fear that it be used to lessen their members' loyalty. This has been particularly true where unions are relatively weak, as in the United States. The powerful Swedish unions have taken a more favorable attitude toward it, while Japanese enterprise unions have not been in a position to resist QWL programs even if they had wanted to do so.

This chapter will concentrate on the QWL experience of Sweden, Japan, and the United States. The movement has spread most widely in the first two nations, while in the United States some very large enterprises have experimented with it. QWL has not been confined to these three countries. The Philips Company in the Netherlands and the German automobile companies have made use of QWL, although in Germany all industrial relations innovations tend to revolve around codetermination. But the three countries chosen for emphasis here illustrate the achievements and drawbacks of QWL.

SWEDEN

Swedish QWL is a composite of government regulation and private agreement. The unions backed governmental action while employers took the lead in the collective bargaining sphere.

The Work Environment Act of 1978 contains detailed regulations on employer responsibilities for safeguarding the safety and health of employees. Employers must adapt working conditions to human physical and mental capabilities and arrange work so that the employees themselves can influence the work situation. Atmospheric, acoustical, and light conditions must be of satisfactory quality. Adequate safeguards to cope with dangerous substances are mandatory, including personal protective equipment. Employers must make sure that employees have a sound knowledge of any risks involved. Many other provisions are also spelled out in detail.

One key section of the law relates to safety delegates. Every establishment with five or more employees must have such an official, who is elected from among the employees for a three-year term. Larger firms have more than one delegate, of whom there are about 110,000 in the entire country. The delegate participates in planning for new premises, processes, and materials; he or she is entitled to all relevant information. If a job appears to involve immediate and serious danger to the life or health of an employee and the employer is not prepared to take corrective action, the delegate may order the work suspended, pending determination by a government labor inspector. The delegate cannot be held personally liable for any damages resulting from suspension.

Establishments with more than fifty employees are required to set up joint management-employee safety committees on which the employees must have one more representative than the employer has. The committees supervise working environment activities and provide the necessary guidelines. About two-thirds of all Swedish employees have access to occupational health services. These are provided by the employer on a voluntary basis with assistance from the government in the form of grants covering up to one-third of the cost. These services are spelled out in detailed agreements between the national organizations of labor and management. The health centers that dispense the services may be restricted to one company or cover several smaller firms. They are administered jointly by labor and management with the assistance of health technicians. They stress the prevention of occupational disease, including psychological problems, rather than the cure. Experts attached to the centers may carry out investigations on their own initiative. Health check-ups are not routinely provided. Attention is concentrated instead on groups of employees who are known to have been exposed to harmful environmental conditions.

This aspect of Swedish QWL seems to work well. When it first came into operation, employers feared that the safety delegates would interrupt work frequently and without adequate cause. To help prevent this, they have cooperated with the unions in a training program that includes a basic 40-hour course. Advanced training is provided if the particular environment of an enterprise requires it, on the recommendation of the safety committee.

Health and safety precautions are found in all industrial countries, but the Swedish system is notable for two things: the power of the safety delegate to stop work and the broad authority of the safety committee. The usual situation elsewhere is for the shop steward (if the plant is organized) to bring complaints to supervisory officials. If the latter consider the complaints groundless, the only recourse for the union is to file grievances or to submit the problem to government labor inspectors. In the meantime, employees must continue to work at their jobs if so directed by supervisors. Health and safety activities are thus normally the exclusive domain of management, though in some countries, Germany for example, works councils may have a voice in company health administration. These differences may not seem of much practical importance. To workers faced with machines or materials that they fear may endanger their health, however, the Swedish system can seem very attractive. As a footnote, safety and health matters have been a prolific source of bitter labor controversy in the United States in recent years.

The second aspect of Swedish QWL has to do primarily with the arrangement of work. Volvo, the automobile firm that employs about 6 percent of the nation's manufacturing labor force and provides 12 percent of its exports, has gained an international reputation for its experiments in work design. This interest derived from growing discontent with straight assembly line work. High absenteeism and turnover resulted in rising production costs. This eventually led to labor-management cooperation that aimed at "humanizing" work through job enlargement and enrichment by replacing the short and repetitive work cycles of traditional production methods. An agreement with the unions was reached in 1982. It called for joint efforts to further QWL activities of this nature.

Even earlier, however, the company had been planning a new approach to automobile production. This approach was first realized in the construction of a new plant in the small town of Kalmar, a name that has since become well known. The plant was built in the form of four hexagons fitted together in a single structure. The center of the building is used for storing materials. Each of the corners made possible by the design is fitted out as an independent assembly shop manned by groups of fifteen to twenty workers. Each group has its own changing room and lounge; all the shops have access to outside light.

Car body parts are brought to an assembly unit by wagons that are guided by magnetic tracks embedded in the floor. When a wagon reaches its destination, it stops automatically and can be parked. This feature enables each group to determine its own work tempo. It can work fast and take longer breaks or work at a more leisurely rate and reduce break time. The most important innovation is the lengthening of the work cycle. Each group member can perform operations taking anywhere from twenty to thirty minutes. Jobs can be interchanged among members of the group. The main limiting condition is that each day the group must deliver a specified number of car doors, brake systems, transmissions, or whatever its production task may be. The group conducts its own quality check, although there is also a separate test station later in the cycle. There the test results are put on television screens and flashed back to the group to alert it of any recurring problems.

Establishing the groups was not without its difficulties. The composition of each group varies in terms of age, sex, and the presence of handicapped individuals. Some groups may like recorded music when they work; others prefer quiet. Differences of opinion are usually decided by majority vote, and transfers may be necessary for people who do not fit in. The presence of women in a group is generally felt to be a stabilizing factor, leading to greater mutual assistance. A wider age spread appears to work better than a narrow one.

Problems have arisen from the necessity of temporarily moving workers from one group to another because of absenteeism. The transferee is often assigned the least interesting work and may feel like a stranger. One way of overcoming this problem is to provide extra compensation to workers who are willing to join a pool from which temporary assignments can be made.

The system does not give workers unlimited job freedom. The quantity of output required is determined by negotiation between management and the union. But workers do have considerable control in deciding who does what as well as the pace of work. Discussions take place within and between groups on how best to arrange the jobs that must be done. Rapid feedback of information on quality enables the group to determine the causes of defects and to make corrections.

Worker reaction has generally been favorable. Of equal importance is that this novel system of work arrangement is feasible from an economic point of view. The Kalmar plant cost 10 percent more to build than a conventional plant of equal capacity, but the extra cost was partly offset by a reduction in the number of supervisors and less absenteeism and turnover. Assembly time proved to be lower than in a conventional plant. As Per Gyllenhammar, the president of Volvo, has pointed out: "The assumption when we started was that the productivity of Kalmar could equal that of any comparable traditional plant. This has proved to be true. More important, this kind of plant has no built-in limits to increased productivity. Thus, we can hope for greater productivity in the future."[1]

In seeking a better quality of working life, Volvo's experiments have not been without risks. A great deal of money was invested in building new plants and reorganizing old ones. Yet Volvo has remained a profitable enterprise despite its small size and its place in an extremely competitive industry. It has been able to market its fairly high-priced cars abroad because of a reputation for quality. There is a general belief in Sweden that a pleasanter working environment has contributed to this end.

JAPAN

The QWL movement in Japan originated in quality control techniques imported from the United States. These developed into so-called quality circles (QC) in the early 1960s and spread rapidly among large enterprises. The initial emphasis was on productivity, but it has since broadened to include other aspects of work.

Kaoru Ishikawa, the Japanese pioneer of the movement, has defined a QC as "a small group which voluntarily . . . performs quality control activities within a single workshop. Moreover, this small group is a continuing organization, within company-wide quality control activities, for mutual self–development and process control and improvement within their workshop utilizing control techniques with full participation of all members."[2] Groups average about eight members each and hold hour–long meetings twice a month. About one–third of the meetings are held after working hours, in which case the participants are either paid overtime or receive meals or education allowances. Company–wide meetings of all QCs are held once or twice a year. It has been estimated that the annual cost per person of meetings, including allowances, was about 10,000 yen, while the direct annual economic benefits realized per person amounted to 150,000 yen.[3] The QCs are thus very profitable.

In addition to their contribution to the improvement of quality, the QCs are intended to contribute to productivity and employee morale in other ways as well. They are supposed to pay attention to plant safety and to reveal employee views on product cost to management. The QC is also believed to promote harmonious personal relationships within the group. Individual suggestions are more easily recognized than through a suggestion box system, and they provide a basis for promotion. The QC concept is applied not only to production, but also to maintenance, material handling, office work, and sales.

The enterprise unions are not involved in the QCs. They approve of them because QCs contribute to profitability and to the ultimate benefit of employees. "Therefore, although it is true that QC circles were initiated and diffused through the support of management, unions fully realize the substantial benefits of such activities which workers may gain."[4] In 1982, a survey of union officials revealed that only a small minority felt that QCs resulted in an intensification of work or made workers more competitive with one another, while more than half believed that they improved communications and human relations. Overall, some 56 percent supported QCs, 42 percent took a neutral position, while less than 2 percent opposed them.

Japanese management has shown little interest in the kinds of work enrichment schemes introduced in Sweden. One reason may lie in the fact that under the Japanese permanent tenure system, employees receive fairly broad training within a job cluster, which means that there is already some job enlargement. One automobile company has engaged in some experimentation, "but remains unconvinced of the value of the Volvo system because of its slight impact on productivity and the required increase in the initial inventory of parts."[5] This difference between the attitudes of successful Japanese and Swedish firms is interesting and merits closer examination. The variables that may be involved include the degree of employee commitment to each firm, satisfaction with traditional job methods, and the means employees have at their disposal to question practices that do not meet with their approval.

Whatever the impact of the QCs on the quality of working life, it is an article of faith in Japan that they are essential to maintaining a high level of productivity. International productivity comparisons are notoriously difficult to make, but few would question the fact that Japan's rising productivity has made a major contribution to the country's economic growth. The precise contribution of QCs has not been quantified and would probably defy measurement efforts, but this does not diminish Japanese enthusiasm for the practice.

THE UNITED STATES

Although the QWL movement has stirred considerable interest in American management circles, it has not yet progressed very far. The obstacles to wider adoption lie on both sides of the bargaining table. Management is concerned lest QWL escalate into greater authority for employees, while the unions see it as a potential management tool for moving toward a union–free environment.

It is not surprising that the greatest interest in QWL has shown up at General Motors and Ford, the giant automobile companies. They are among the firms hardest hit by Japanese competition and have been impressed by the apparent contribution of QCs to Japanese productivity. Like Japanese employers, their interest has been primarily in the productivity potential of QWL rather than in the Swedish safety and design approach.[6]

GM's interest was spurred by rising dissatisfaction among its employees in the early 1970s, which culminated in a wildcat strike at its Lordstown, Ohio, plant in 1972. The GM management and the United Automobile Workers (UAW) agreed to establish a national committee to look into the possibilities of QWL. Progress was slow; by 1979, only six of the twenty-two plants in GM's body division were involved. An economic recession led to more adoptions, but even then, only four of the plants had a majority of hourly workers engaged in some form of QWL activity.

QWL in the GM empire primarily took the form of QCs that met for about an hour a week on company time. The focus was on quality, but the groups also discussed such housekeeping matters as lighting and ventilation. There was no immediate tendency to move into such broader issues as revising working rules or rearranging work patterns. During this initial phase of the movement, a survey of GM plants revealed that there was a small but significant improvement in product quality, but no finding of any positive effect on labor efficiency, absenteeism, or the number of grievances filed by the union.

GM began to widen the scope of its QWL program in the 1960s, particularly in new plants. Operating teams of ten to fifteen workers have been set up, and the jobs of team members have been broadened. The teams are entrusted with inspections and repair, as in Volvo. In some plants, the teams perform housekeeping and machine maintenance and cooperate in job design. However, GM has not gone in for the new structural forms introduced by Volvo.

The Ford Motor Company entered the QWL movement in the 1980s. In 1987, Ford entered into an agreement with the UAW that looked toward a cooperative effort to improve product quality and productivity. A joint National Job Security and Operational Effectiveness Committee was formed to direct and assist similar committees at the plant level. All the committees are supposed to examine the need for new investment in facilities, to establish production teams, to identify possible nonlabor cost savings, to consider new forms of work planning, and of course to raise quality standards. It remains to be seen how the agreement will be implemented. Not to be outdone, GM signed a similar agreement, and Chrysler followed suit. The American automobile industry seems to be headed into deeper involvement with QWL with the cooperation of the union.

QWL experiments have occurred in other industries as well. One of the most ambitious was undertaken jointly by the American Telephone and Telegraph Co. and the Communications Workers of America. After an auspicious start, the project was derailed when AT&T was broken up into independent components after marathon antitrust litigation.[7] Xerox and the Amalgamated Clothing Workers agreed upon a program that was slow in getting started but has persisted. Similar initiatives in the steel industry, however, fell victim to plant closures and a sharp drop in output.

The attitude of American trade unions toward QWL has ranged from cooperation to complete rejection. When unions suspect that QWL is a means of weakening the solidarity of their members, they naturally oppose it. Cooperation is possible primarily when employers accept the legitimacy of unions and do not seek to displace them. This was clearly expressed by Thomas R. Donohue, the secretary-treasury of the AFL-CIO:

For strong unions, able to insist on an equal and active voice in how the program works, or able, if necessary, to veto actions that aim at subverting its bargaining position, QWL isn't an insuperable problem. That accounts for the general acceptance of worklife programs by such dominant and secure unions as the Auto Workers, Steel Workers, and Communications Workers. Even they have sometimes had to take strong action to prevent their employers from using the programs as conduits for company propaganda in bargaining situations.[8]

The QWL movement in the United States now stands at a crossroads. Unions might find QWL more palatable if there were greater stress on making work more comfortable and less on raising productivity. On the other hand, some employers fear that QWL is an entering wedge to augment employee power at the plant level.

The success of QWL in Sweden derives from the high degree of union-management consensus that prevails there. QCs prosper in Japan because employers find them useful. The strongly adversarial nature of American industrial relations and the refusal of many employers to accept the unionization of their employees place the future of QWL in the United States in question.

The QWL movement is by no means confined to Sweden, Japan, and the United States. Both the federal and provincial governments in Canada have taken an active interest in it. A new Fiat plant built at Cassino embodies some of the Volvo technology, but Italian unions have not been cordial to the productivity aspects of QWL. The German government has sponsored a work humanization program, but works council legislation makes it difficult to set up small autonomous groups of workers. In France, QWL has been hampered by suspicion on the part of the ideological and weak trade unions. Norway was the birthplace of QWL, and the Philips Corporation in the Netherlands was one of the first large companies to welcome it.

In Europe, Sweden has taken the lead. Relatively more workers are involved in QWL in Japan than in any other country, but the focus there differs from that in Europe. The United States is in the process of making up its mind about the whole idea, with much depending on the ability of the labor movement to turn back a decade-long employer offensive and regain some of its former economic power.

NOTES

1. Per Gyllenhammar, *People at Work* (London: Addison-Wesley Publishing, 1977), p. 69.

2. Kaoru Ishikawa, *Quality Control Circles at Work* (Tokyo: Asian Productivity Organization, 1984), p. 4.

3. Takeshi Inagami, *Labor-Management Communication at the Workshop Level* (Tokyo: Japan Institute of Labor, 1983), p. 32.

4. *Ibid.*, p. 33.

5. Kazutoshi Koshiro, "The Quality of Working Life in Japanese Factories." In Taishiro Shirai, ed., *Contemporary Industrial Relations in Japan* (Madison: University of Wisconsin Press, 1983), pp. 74–75.

6. The following account is based on Thomas A. Kochan, Harry C. Katz, and Robert B. McKersie, *The Transformation of American Industrial Relations* (New York: Basic Books, 1986), and on Harry C. Katz, Thomas A. Kochan, and Kenneth Gobeille, "Industrial Relations Performance, Economic Performance, and QWL Programs," *Industrial and Labor Relations Review* (October 1983), p. 3.

7. The initial experience is recounted in U.S. Department of Labor, *Quality of Work Life: AT & T and CWA Examine Process After Three Years* (Washington: GPO, 1985).

8. Quoted in Thomas Kochan, Harry Katz, and Nancy R. Mower, *Worker Participation and American Unions* (Kalamazoo, Mich.: Upjohn Institute, 1984), p. 155.

Chapter Four

EMPLOYMENT TENURE

Higher wages and shorter working hours have been the traditional goals of trade unions from their very inception. As workers became more affluent, better working conditions were added to the list, but insecurity of employment was accepted as a characteristic of capitalism. Employers could not be expected to maintain a peak labor force during the downswings of the inevitable business cycle. Measures were adopted to cushion the shock of discharge, primarily in the form of unemployment benefits that were first set up by unions and eventually taken over by governments. Employers were held responsible for unemployment only to the minor extent reflected in merit-rated unemployment compensation schemes. The idea that they could be expected to provide permanent jobs was regarded as utopian.

As the result of several developments, the emphasis of worker concerns and union demands is shifting to security of employment. The first development is the combination of rising money wages and high marginal income tax rates. Particularly in the welfare states of Northern Europe, where governments are preempting increasing shares of the national income to finance welfare schemes, employees have learned that higher money wages before taxes can become lower real wages after taxes and price inflation. A larger pay packet is no longer the principal measure of union success. The money illusion is gone.

A second development is the structural transformation that Western economies are undergoing. The decline of manufacturing employment—not output, but employment—has meant that many blue-collar workers are permanently displaced. They have the option to retire from the labor force or to retrain for service jobs that often pay less than the manufacturing jobs that have disappeared. Retaining a foothold in the manufacturing sector is becoming a matter of greater importance than higher wages or shorter hours.

The recent emphasis that European unions have placed on reducing working hours may seem to contradict this proposition, but in fact it does not. With unemployment rates rising to double-digit levels in some countries, labor organizations have adopted the theory that spreading the available work through shorter hours is the best way to protect employment tenure. This theory has questionable validity. Reducing working hours may be desirable for social reasons, but it is not likely to preserve employment.

For these and other reasons, permanency of employment may well become the major working life objective of the twenty-first century. In fact, a substantial number of people in developed countries already enjoy a considerable degree of employment security. This would be true of most government employees: in Sweden, one-third of the labor force falls into this category; in France, Britain, and a number of other countries, about 20 percent of workers do. The United States and Germany lag behind at about 15 percent, with Japan still further down at 6.5 percent.

High-security jobs are not confined to the government sector. Teachers and staff in many schools in the United States, private as well as public, enjoy what amounts to employment tenure. Senior employees of large firms that operate under union contract can usually count on staying with their firms except in the event of bankruptcy or the closure of entire plants. There are other pockets of secure jobs throughout the economy, which magnifies the contrast between those who can count on satisfactory work opportunities until they retire and those who constantly face the prospect of unemployment.

JAPAN

In the Japanese system, rising concern with job security has led to great interest in what is variously termed "lifetime employment" or "permanent commitment." In the ideal conception of the system, an enterprise hires all employees directly from school, blue-collar workers from secondary schools and skilled white-collar employees from colleges. After a probationary period that may last as long as year, the employee receives tenured status. He will then be discharged only for such reasons as excessive absenteeism, behavior detrimental to the company's reputation, or the commission of crimes. An employee is not subject to discharge or even temporary layoff if a decline in business renders his services superfluous or if his work is not up to standard.

An integral part of the system is the use of seniority as the major factor in wage determination. The implication is that wage rates are determined by age, length of service, and education, thus guaranteeing a positive lifetime income curve. This practice tends to encourage loyalty to the firm and to discourage interfirm mobility. Every tenured employee can look forward to a lifetime of rising compensation, regardless of performance.

This is the ideal system. There are, however, many exceptions and loopholes when it comes to its actual operation. Among them are the following:

1. *Coverage.* There are no accurate figures on the proportion of Japanese employees who are covered by the lifetime employment commitment, a surprising fact in view of the existence of excellent data relating to most other aspects of Japanese working life. A recent publication of the U.S. Department of Labor puts the figure at "no more than the top 10–15 percent of the work force."[1] While this figure is probably on the low side, there is no argument about the fact that the system prevails mainly in the largest firms. Most firms whose products have become household words in America and Europe would fall into this category, as well those in basic steel and shipbuilding.

2. *Temporary and subcontract workers.* Not all employees of the larger firms enjoy lifetime tenure. Only those on the regular tenure track who are recruited directly from school are normally within the system. Most larger firms employ temporary workers hired directly from the labor market for relatively short periods. In addition, a good deal of work is subcontracted out, often to contractors who work for one company only. Temporary and subcontract employees receive no employment guarantee and are generally ineligible for membership in the enterprise union; they are certainly not required to join it.

This discrimination among employees is an important element in making the system economically viable. In the event of a business downturn, the fringe labor force can be laid off first. This practice has a parallel in that followed in the past by some European countries of laying off "guest workers" (aliens who held temporary work permits) before letting citizens go when the demand for labor slackened. This has not been a permanent feature of the European labor market, however.

3. *Women.* Although many large firms recruit women directly from school, they do not generally accord them the status of lifetime employees. Women are expected to leave their employment with these firms when they reached marriageable age in their mid-twenties, even if they do not get married. A recent article has summed up their employment status:

Women are not guaranteed lifetime employment, nor do they enjoy the benefits of the seniority wage systems since they are regarded as marginal labor. . . . Women are employed as part-time workers in much the same way the small and middle scale companies are used as subcontractors.[2]

If women eventually return to their old firms, they do so as nonpermanent employees. However, the rising proportion of women in the labor force—they now constitute about 36 percent of wage and salary earners—and the enactment in 1986 of an Equal Employment Opportunity law may eventually help to break the male monopoly of permanent employment.

4. *Turnover.* Not all men who join a lifetime employment firm remain permanently. The average monthly separation rate in Japanese manufacturing has been between 1 and 2 percent, half the rate in the United States. As one might expect, turnover is highest among younger workers who may not find the work to which they have been assigned to their liking. While much of such separation is voluntary, it is not always easy to draw the line between voluntary and involuntary leaving. Japanese managers are skillful at easing out undesirable employees. Transfer to a more arduous job or to a new location is a method sometimes used to induce resignation.

As employees grow older, it becomes more difficult for them to change employment. This is a universal phenomenon, but in Japan there is an added obstacle in the reluctance of large firms to hire mid-career workers. A man who leaves a regular job with a large firm is more or less restricted to less secure employment with smaller firms, unless he possesses a skill that another large firm badly needs. To the security-minded Japanese, loss of a lifetime job can be a catastrophe.

5. *Retirees.* Another cost-reducing element is the retirement system. The compulsory retirement age for regular employees was fifty-five

until recently. At present, some 85 percent of firms with 5,000 or more employees have raised the retirement age to sixty years. Because pensions are generally inadequate, most retirees continue to work. Some are taken on by their old companies in subordinate positions at lower pay, while others find work elsewhere. The Japanese situation may be compared with that in the United States, where mandatory retirement at any age will soon be illegal. Despite the fact that Japan leads the world in longevity of life, its relatively early retirement age reduces the potential cost of the employment guarantee. The term "lifetime commitment" is a misnomer if taken literally.

Despite all the cushions surrounding the system of permanent employment, redundancy cannot always be avoided. The Japanese economy has been undergoing the same structural adjustments as those of Western nations. What do Japanese firms do when there is simply no work available for their permanent staff? The answer is that they have shown remarkable ingenuity in forestalling any breakdown of the system. A few examples will illustrate the measures that have been adopted.[3]

1. Japan's largest steel company, Nippon Steel, unveiled a plan in 1987 to shut down five of its twelve blast furnaces. The labor force in steel-making was to be reduced by 19,000 persons by the end of 1990. Of these redundant employees, it was estimated that 9,000 would retire or leave for personal reasons, 6,000 would be transferred to the company's non-steel operations, and 4,000 would be transferred to subsidiaries or laid off temporarily.

2. The second largest steel firm, Nippon Kokan, planned to reduce its work force by 8,000, a quarter of its total èmployment. This was to be accomplished by 2,500 retirements and 5,500 transfers to subsidiaries or new projects.

Japanese enterprises thus have a free hand in moving their employees from one job to another; no jurisdictional boundaries impede internal mobility. Permanent employees must be prepared to accept relocation even if it means finding new homes. Occasionally, redundant employees have been temporarily lent or hired out to other enterprises. If all else fails, employees may be laid off temporarily at an allowance of 80 to 90 percent of their wages, a substantial proportion of which is subsidized by government grants. It was estimated, for example, that during the 1975 recession government subsidies saved 300,000 jobs, at a time when a million workers were unemployed in the economy as a whole at some time during the year.[4] But these wage subsidies, which are financed by a payroll tax, do not go directly to the workers, but rather through company channels: "semantics are extremely important in this connection: in Japan, no one dares associate the scheme with unemployment, a taboo word to the Japanese. The payments are for 'employment stabilization,' not for income maintenance for the unemployed."[5]

While there have been no wholesale layoffs of permanent employees, firms have been increasing the ratio of part–time and temporary workers to their total staff. As a Japanese observer has noted, "The coexistence of decreasing core workers on the one hand and increasing flexible workers on the other is a key for understanding the changing structure of today's labor market in Japan. The labor market is certainly in the process of substantial transformation."[6]

Despite structural and other problems, the lifetime employment system appears to have remained basically intact. Firms retain a great deal of flexibility in adjusting to necessary employment shifts, which is a big plus for efficiency. Core employees are apt to be the most productive by virtue of the training that they have received during long association with their companies. They may be dissatisfied with particular attributes of their jobs—wages, equipment, or working conditions—but they appear to have a strong concern for the viability of their enterprises.

The docility of Japanese trade unions, as manifested by the absence of strikes among other things, derives largely from the lifetime employment system. Union members appear to have been willing to forego the advantages of full–time, professional, outside representation in return for the employment guarantee. They see nothing wrong with working alongside nonunion temporary employees in order to maintain their favored positions. The basic ideology of Japanese enterprise unionism rests squarely on the employment system. If the employment commitment should falter, profound changes could occur in trade union structure and function. A more aggressive stance might very probably follow. The large firms thus have a strong incentive to maintain the system intact.

In sum, lifetime commitment is a key aspect of Japanese labor market organization. Although limited in scope to a minority of the labor force, in the salient sectors where it is in effect firms have received major benefits at relatively small cost. There is little doubt about this system's rationality from an economic standpoint. Japanese custom and tradition may have contributed to its adoption and continuing strength, but the efficiency criterion alone should be sufficient to sustain its popularity with Japanese management.

GREAT BRITAIN

The Japanese employment system is unique. In no other country has so large a proportion of the labor force been able to remain with the same enterprises for the duration of their working lives. However, other countries have also adopted measures designed either to protect jobs by making layoffs difficult or to provide compensation to employees for the loss of jobs in which they have invested substantial periods of time.

The British have pursued such a course. The present system was initiated by the Redundancy Payments (RP) Act of 1965 and amended in 1978. Its original purpose was to secure the cooperation of workers in facilitating the transfer of labor from declining to expanding industries. The theory of the legislation was that workers would be more likely to accept layoffs without protest if they received financial compensation for what they might have come to regard as property rights in their jobs. The cost was to be spread across all industry rather than concentrated in the declining industries that were least able to bear it.

The legislation provides that employees with a minimum of two years of service with the same employer may be entitled to lump sum payments if they are laid off for economic reasons. The employer may offer alternative suitable employment, and the employee may lose the right to benefits if he refuses it without just cause. If the new employment differs from the old, the employee is entitled to a trial period of at least four weeks to determine the suitability of the new employment.

For each year of service, employees between the ages of eighteen and twenty-one years are entitled to half a week's pay; for those between twenty-one and forty years, a full week's pay; and for those between forty-one and sixty-five years (sixty years for women), one-and-a-half week's pay. There is a maximum of thirty weeks of pay and also a cap on compensable pay levels, which has been adjusted annually since 1978. Persons employed less than sixteen hours a week do not qualify for benefits unless they have at least five years of continuous employment at eight hours a week or more.

A national fund was established to subsidize the payments. It is financed by levies on both employers and employees. An employer who makes a redundancy payment receives a rebate of 35 percent from the fund. If he pays more than the statutory minimum based on a private agreement, the fund will reimburse only for the statutory amount.

The benefits paid by employers and the fund have been substantial. From 1966 to 1984, a total of 6.6 million payments were made. Up to 1979, the average annual number of payments was about a quarter of a million. The subsequent economic depression raised the number to a peak of 800,000 in 1981, with a decline thereafter. The fund was supposed to be self-financing but in fact it has had to resort to borrowing for about half its life.[7]

The RP scheme was supplemented in 1975 by the Employment Protection Act. Among other things, this act stipulates that if an employer plans to dismiss between ten and ninety-nine people, he must give at least thirty days prior notice to the unions representing the employees. The notice period rises to sixty days if more than a hundred people are affected. The reasons for the dismissals must be specified as well as the method of selecting those to be dismissed.

What was not anticipated when the RP scheme was enacted was the extent to which it would be supplemented by voluntary agreements. Some 90 percent of a sample of agreements analyzed in 1984 provided for payments higher than the statutory amounts; half of them paid twice as much, and more than one-quarter tripled the statutory limit. For older, long-service employees, this could mean more than a year of pre-dismissal pay.

Workers have apparently been less reluctant to accept dismissal than had been expected. Layoffs had been a prolific source of strikes prior to the enactment of the scheme. In the face of the willingness of workers to accept compensated dismissal, even those unions that had been skeptical have had difficulty in adopting a more militant stance. What they have done instead is to negotiate for more generous payments.

What proportion of the separations has been voluntary is not known. It has probably varied with the generosity of the benefits. Linking payments to age has made older workers more likely to volunteer for dismissal, which is in accord with management preferences. In the normal course of events, not all volunteers are accepted; management sometimes indicates that applications will not be accepted from specific groups, particularly the skilled. An employee may quit his job without management concurrence, of course, but in that event he loses the right to redundancy benefits. When there are insufficient volunteers, seniority is likely to be the criterion for selection.

The RP scheme has been in operation for a sufficiently long time to permit fairly firm conclusions about its operation:

1. Voluntary resignation has been more frequent than mandatory selection of workers to be laid off. The ratio has been two to one in the presence of strong unions; the reverse is true in nonunion situations.

2. The scheme appears to have reduced opposition to layoffs among workers because it has lessened the fear of economic insecurity during spells of unemployment. However, there is little evidence that its original purpose—channeling workers from declining to expanding industries—has been achieved. One of the problems has been that a disproportionate number of those laid off were older people who were least suited for retraining.

3. Spreading the cost of redundancy benefits over the entire business community has been achieved only in part. Payments above the statutory level have had to be borne entirely by the dismissing firm. The blow is softened, however, by allowing such payments to be written off against taxes. It has been estimated that employers in general bear about 18 percent of the benefit costs while employers directly involved in the layoffs pay 54 percent; the rest comes from employee contributions to the national fund.

4. Employers appear to be satisfied with the scheme. It has enhanced their freedom to adjust the size of their labor force without running into employee and community opposition. Two-thirds of employees laid off receive benefits, with the remainder being disqualified for insufficient length of service or for some other reason.

5. There has been a drastic reduction of employment in declining industries without much industrial strife, but this may have been achieved by stimulating early retirement rather than by RP benefits.

6. The RP system does not appear to have deterred the recruitment of new employees, nor to have led to the loss of key workers.

7. The 1975 legislation requiring advance notification of layoffs appears to have had little effect on the ability of employers to bring about staff reductions. This may be due in part to the coexistence of the RP scheme which makes careful advance planning for layoffs necessary.[8]

From some points of view, RP appears to have contributed to job insecurity rather than security. It removes some pressure on employers to maintain employment and makes it easier for employees to leave their jobs. Still, it may enhance economic security by assuring employees that they are accumulating employment equities that can be cashed in if jobs disappear. This is a far cry from lifetime tenure, but it does mean that long years of employment cannot simply be terminated without anything to show for them.

Redundancy compensation is not the only way in which British employers are encouraged to maintain employment and to make the transition from work to unemployment easier; other ways will be considered in the next chapter. It should also be pointed out that severance pay is by no means unique to Britain. What makes the British system different is the combination of government and private support for the scheme and the fact that benefits are mandatory. The idea that jobs confer property rights upon those who hold them has become a practical reality.

GERMANY

The first line of defense against mass layoffs in Germany is advance notification. Any employer that anticipates dismissing employees within the following twelve month period is required to report these intentions to the regional Department of Employment, together with the reaction of its works council. Failure to do so may oblige the employer to pay for retraining or placement of the displaced employees.

A dismissal becomes effective only after a month's notice to the Department of Employment. During this so-called status quo period, a tripartite local or regional commission considers the matter and may extend the status quo for a second month if it affords the employees a better chance of finding new work. The commissions usually consult management and the works councils. They may attempt to avert the layoff by arranging for government financial assistance to firms that find themselves in temporary difficulties. The manner in which this arrangement works varies a good deal from area to area, but at least it provides a breathing spell.

More important is the possibility of action under the codetermination system. The works council must be informed in advance of projected plant closures, mergers, or any other development that may result in employee problems. The council may then demand a "social plan" to minimize the negative impact. The details of the plan are negotiated between management and the council. If they cannot agree, the plan is submitted to a tripartite arbitration commission for final determination. As a safeguard, no decision can place "an unreasonable financial burden" on the firm.

Almost all plans have been negotiated in connection with full or partial plant closures.[9] For larger enterprises, transfers to other plants are the preferred solution. These firms are often interested in holding on to younger and better qualified workers, who may forfeit dismissal pay if they refuse transfer. For the rest, monetary compensation is usually given to those who are laid off, based on age and previous earnings. Firms in poor financial straits normally pay less than do those that are better off. The plans may also cover such fringe benefits as the right to continue living in company-owned housing, private pensions, earned vacation allowances, continuation of profit-sharing benefits for a specified period, and Christmas bonuses. When employees must move to new workplaces, they may receive limited payments to cover lost income as well as moving costs. It is important to note that the specific terms of the social plans are not mandated by legislation. The result is that there is no uniform level of compensation for dismissals.

Agreements to protect employees against adverse effects caused by the introduction of new technology are also part of German job protection. About half of all employees are covered by them. Transfers and retraining are the principal methods used. Many agreements bar the dismissal of employees over specified ages or years of service because of technological change. Works councils must be consulted well in advance of such changes, although they cannot stop them.

When dismissals are shown to be necessary, the criteria for selecting specific individuals to be laid off are generally determined by labor-management agreements. The relative weights given to the employees' personal situations and to employer interests vary, but the former are always taken into consideration.

Job protection in Germany depends largely on the firm involved: its size, financial resources, and degree of trade union influence. In large, profitable firms such as Volkswagen, outright dismissals are a last resort after all other means to save jobs have been tried. Government financial assistance and short-term wage subsidies may be available to bolster a firm's own resources. In smaller firms, particularly those without works councils, the protection afforded employees is much weaker. Firms with fewer than twenty employees can implement layoffs summarily. One of the goals of the German trade unions is to extend the social plan requirement to all firms.

By all accounts, works council intervention has succeeded in reducing controversy over dismissals and in bringing broader social considerations into plant closures. It has been argued, however, that this very success may have adverse effects on employment by making enterprises cautious about hiring new staff. Some employers have been able to shield themselves from the full impact of the dismissal procedure by resorting to types of employment that fall outside the protective network: part-time work, short-term contracts with an automatic termination date, temporary labor from employment agencies, or subcontracting. Still, given the safeguards built into the system and the propensity to negotiate reasonable solutions to labor market controversies characteristic of present-day Germany, it would be difficult to support the proposition that the employment protection procedures now in effect have had a negative impact on the efficiency of German industry.

FRANCE

The French system of employment protection is based on a combination of legislation and national collective bargaining contracts. Agreements reached in 1969 and amended in 1974 stipulated that when a firm was contemplating a layoff, it was obliged to notify the local works committee and to supply it with information regarding the number and categories of workers to be laid off. It also had to propose a "social plan" covering projected transfers, training, reemployment rights, and retirement offers. These plans could be modified after discussion with the works committees. A substantial number of such plans have been adopted, concentrating mainly on early retirement, retraining, and assistance to employees in finding other jobs.

For some years, employers had been obliged to secure the permission of local Labor Department officials before effectuating layoffs. The officials had the authority to prevent the layoffs if they felt them to be unwarranted. This requirement was repealed in 1986 over strenuous trade union objection. Employers had complained that it could take from four to twelve months to lay off redundant workers; they argued that the result was a reluctance to rehire when business picked up.

Statutory employment protection has also been provided in another form. Legislation enacted in 1985 set up a new type of benefit, a "job conversion" allowance, financed by a National Employment Fund. Eligibility is restricted to employees of firms that had entered into agreements with the Ministry of Labor and to employees who voluntarily agree to accept job conversion leave when offered by the employer. Virtually all large firms have signed up. The minimum length of this leave period is set at four months, and the maximum that the government will help to finance is limited to ten months. The employee retains his employment status during the leave period and is entitled to 65 percent of his gross average earnings during the previous year, with the Employment Fund bearing half the cost.

While on leave, the employee may attend courses of study to acquire new skills that the employer may need, particularly in advanced technologies. If the employee fails to find work by the end of the leave period, he may be dismissed, in which case he receives normal unemployment benefits *retroactive* to the beginning of his job conversion leave.

This legislation was supplemented by the Act of December, 1986, which covers layoffs of fewer than ten employees where social plans are not required. In such cases, the employer must offer a job conversion contract to each employee with a minimum of two years service. If the employee accepts, his employment status is deemed to be terminated by mutual accord rather than by layoff. The contract has a duration of five months, during which the employee receives an allowance equal to 70 percent of his previous earnings, financed jointly by the Employment Fund, the unemployment insurance system, and the employer. The period of contract duration is presumably to be used for training and job search.

These job conversion schemes are essentially redundancy payments, but they impose some responsibility on the employer for helping employees to find new jobs, particularly in the case of those whose skills must be upgraded. It is too early to determine how well the system has been working or whether the Socialist government that came into office in 1988 will be satisfied to leave things as they are. The government faced a problem of high unemployment throughout the late 1980s that was not alleviated by the new hirings that employers had predicted would result from the 1986 change in the redundancy rules. The trade unions would like to see a reinstatement of the administrative permission requirement for economic dismissals, but this does not appear likely.

THE UNITED STATES

The employment protection situation in the United States was well summarized in a report by the General Accounting Office to a Congressional committee in 1987. A survey of plant closures during 1983 and 1984 revealed that about 16,200 business establishments with fifty or more employees either closed or experienced permanent layoffs during these years, resulting in 1.3 million jobs lost. Over half of these establishments had been doing business at the same sites for fifteen years or more. Only a relatively small number went into bankruptcy.

Two-thirds of these establishments that had 100 or more employees provided less than fifteen days advance notice of closure or discharge to their employees. A third provided no notice at all, while 5 percent gave more than thirty days notice. More union than nonunion firms gave advance notice, as would be expected. Less than 30 percent offered dismissed employees some financial or reemployment assistance, most commonly in the form of severance pay, continuation of health and life insurance, and help in job search. Severance pay, transfer options, and time off for job search were more commonly offered to white-collar than blue-collar employees.[10]

A few large firms had adopted practices that almost amounted to a lifetime employment commitment. One of them was IBM, the giant computer company. But in 1986, in the face of slow growth, IBM reduced its employment by offering early retirement, which was accepted by 15,000 employees. Another 1,000 inside employees were offered sales jobs in 1988. Projected plant closures are expected to lead to additional transfers. Direct layoffs appear to have been avoided thus far.

An indication of the importance that American workers attach to job security appears in recent collective agreements between the major automobile companies and the UAW. In return for an employee commitment to raise productivity and improve quality, the Ford Motor Co. has agreed to maintain current job levels in all plants and forego layoffs for any reason except carefully defined reductions in production linked to market conditions. Should employees be laid off, the company agrees to recall them in proportion to any increase in output before it resorts to overtime work. Employees with one year of service are covered by the job protection scheme.

At each plant, a pool of employees who would normally be laid off is to be established. They continue to receive the same rates of pay as they earned before assignment to the pool. They can be placed in a training program or transferred to other work; if they refuse, they are subject to layoff. Senior pool members have the first right to available jobs within their geographical area; if no one in the area accepts the vacancy, it can be offered to employees in other areas.

The company has also pledged itself to give greater weight to job stability before deciding to buy parts from outside firms and to establish joint committees to police this requirement. If agreement cannot be reached locally, the matter is to be submitted to a joint national committee. The union is to receive ninety days notice of any intent to purchase parts from the outside.

An almost identical agreement has been reached with General Motors. In a speech delivered soon after its consummation, the company's executive vice-president revealed something of the philosophy behind this concession to the union:

We in the United States have had to learn some painful lessons from some of our global competitors: that their competitive advantage lies not so much in automation or cultural distinctiveness or a superior work ethic, but primarily in the way the work force is organized and empowered. . . . While I do not hold out any of the Japanese or Swedish manufacturing systems as a moral ideal, the best of them have exposed serious flaws in both our institutional mechanisms and our managerial practices pertaining to the mobilization of human resources.[11]

Chrysler has also followed along. It should be noted that the auto agreements fall far short of a lifetime employment commitment. The firms retain the power to lay workers off if demand declines, a right that they have since exercised on a number of occasions in the face of falling car sales. There is no contractual obligation to compensate workers in such an event.

The UAW gained a stronger guarantee from Case IH, a manufacturer of agricultural equipment. The company agreed to maintain the existing level of employment at six plants for the duration of a three-year contract, subject only to upward or downward revisions resulting from new hiring or normal attrition. In return, the union agreed to more flexible work rules, overtime provisions, and transfer rules. The company has retained the right to shut the plants down for an annual four-week vacation, which can be extended to six weeks if justified by reduced sales.

These examples may be straws in the wind or simply reflect what several large corporations are willing to chance after a number of years of profitable operation. All these employment guarantees terminate with the expiration of the contracts that established them and will have to be renegotiated to continue in effect.

Finally, in 1988 the United States adopted the beginnings of a national employment preservation policy. Congress enacted a law, without the approval of President Reagan, that requires a sixty-day advance notice when a firm plans to dismiss at least fifty people in the course of shutting down an office or factory. Similar notice is required when a firm that plans to continue operating at the same site eliminates at least fifty jobs, provided that these jobs constitute at least one-third of its labor force at that location. The law also applies when 500 or more employees at a particular site are affected, whatever proportion of the labor force they constitute.

Notice is not required if the layoff is caused by "not reasonably foreseeable" circumstances, if sending out a notice would adversely affect the firm's ability to raise capital or attract new business, or if a strike is in progress. It remains to be seen whether this small step in the direction of greater job security, which was strongly opposed by employer groups, along with these broad safeguards, will prove to have any practical significance.

NOTES

1. U.S. Department of Labor, "Japan," *Foreign Labor Trends* (1987–1988), p. 13.

2. Omori Maki, "Women Workers and the Japanese Industrial Relations System." In Joachim Bergmann and Shigeyoshi Tokunaga, eds., *Economic and Social Aspects of Industrial Relations* (Frankfurt: Campus Verlag, 1987), p. 127.

3. These examples come from Japanese Institute of Labor, *Japan Labor Bulletin* (April 1987).

4. Haruo Shimada, *The Japanese Employment System* (Tokyo: Japanese Institute of Labor, 1980), p. 27.

5. Koji Taira, "Japanese Labor Market Policies." In Howard Rosen, ed., *Comparative Labor Policies* (Washington: National Council on Employment Policy, 1986), p. 16.

6. Yasuo Kuwahara, "The Process of Job Creation and Job Destruction in Japanese Industry," *Japan Labor Bulletin* (March 1988).

7. Paul Lewis, *Twenty Years of Statutory Redundancy Payments in Great Britain* (Nottingham, U.K.: Universities of Leeds and Nottingham, 1985), pp. 14–21.

8. The previous observations are based on Paul Lewis, *Twenty Years*; Michael Cross, ed., *Managing Workforce Reduction* (New York: Praeger, 1985); Alan Gordon, *Redundancy in the 1980s* (Aldershot: Gower Publishing, 1984); John Gennard, "Great Britain." In Edward Yemin, *Workforce Reduction in Undertakings* (Geneva: International Labor Office, 1982).

9. Michael Cross, *Managing Workforce Reduction*, pp. 180–184.

10. U.S. General Accounting Office, Report B-223485 (Washington: GPO), April 17, 1987.

11. Speech of Elmer W. Johnson, presented at various universities, Spring 1988.

Chapter Five

REDUCING UNEMPLOYMENT

Despite efforts to preserve jobs, some unemployment is inevitable in a dynamic economy. There is considerable disagreement on an acceptable level. What some economists might regard as a "natural" rate of unemployment, which arises from necessary labor mobility and contributes to economic efficiency, might be considered by others to be intolerably high and to warrant corrective measures by government.

Most countries are formally committed to the achievement of "full" employment, a goal that is not well defined but has a great deal of popular appeal. Politically acceptable levels of unemployment vary not only across countries but also within countries over time. Rates of unemployment that might have driven governments out of office two decades ago might be regarded as unfortunate but inevitable today.

There are at least two broad approaches to the reduction of unemployment: stimulating the economy in an effort to create more jobs and improving the operation of the labor market to secure a better match between the buyers and sellers of labor. The first, usually identified in one way or another with the theories of J. M. Keynes, involves raising demand for goods and services by combinations of increased government spending, reduced taxation, and subsidies to enterprises that find themselves in financial difficulties. This approach was in fashion until the 1970s, when it became clear that demand stimulation could lead to inflation without having much effect on unemployment—so-called stagflation. Rising government budget deficits also made resort to such solutions less appealing.

This situation led governments to pay greater attention to measures to enhance the efficiency of labor markets. The present chapter deals with this area of policy rather than with the more visible attempts at macroeconomic solutions. Various types of programs may contribute to this end and are available to government and to private enterprise. They are well known. It is hardly a secret, for example, that retraining workers whose skills have become obsolete may help them find new jobs. What makes the difference is the amount of resources that a country is prepared to devote to getting people back to work and the quality of the administration to which reemployment is entrusted. It is important to look at systems as a whole rather than at any particular measure.

SWEDEN

No country is more devoted to full employment than Sweden. There is national consensus on the proposition that everyone who wants to work is entitled to a job. In Sweden, a government that permitted unemployment to rise to levels that would be eminently satisfactory in other countries would be committing political suicide. It is this commitment that has given rise to what is known as the Swedish "active labor market policy." Gosta Rehn is an economist and former trade union official who more than any other individual is responsible for the conception and promotion of this approach to the alleviation of unemployment. He summarized it in the following terms:

By an active labor market policy we mean those programs which promote either job creation where labor demand is too low to lead to full employment (demand-oriented programs) or the readjustment of labor to the intersectoral or interarea differences and variances in.the structure of demand (supply-oriented programs). Efforts to promote the simultaneous matching of supply and demand through information and an effective Employment Service also fit the concept.[1]

At the core of the system is the National Labor Market Board, a government agency operating through twenty-four county labor boards and some 290 local employment offices. The National Board is headed by a fifteen-member directorate, nine of whom represent labor and employer organizations. The county boards are also tripartite in composition. It is believed that this structure gives the boards more independence and a greater ability to act quickly than would be the case with unilateral government boards, since the labor market organizations are thus directly involved in the determination and implementation of policy rather than having to exert influence through a roundabout consultative process.

In October 1976, the first nonsocialist government in forty-four years came into office. A number of industries had been affected adversely by a combination of economic recession and the onset of structural adjustment, particularly in steel and shipbuilding, both important industries in Sweden. The government instituted a policy of capital subsidies to firms that were in difficulty, citing the need to protect employment. At their peak in 1982/1983, these subsidies constituted 2.8 percent of the GNP. Most of the enterprises affected were large ones, often located in isolated areas where there were few alternative employment opportunities. The politicians were under great pressure not only to prevent an erosion of employment in general, but also to protect existing jobs where they were located.

This policy did not work. Despite the large sums that were poured into shipyards and steel mills, their employment fell. By 1985, it was far below the 1975 level. It became necessary to abandon subsidies and to allow some enterprises to go into bankruptcy. The cost of supporting employment in this manner was thus too great. Sweden as well as other countries learned the hard way that subsidizing declining industries to protect employment is not feasible.

Alternative policies aimed at improving the efficiency of the labor market consisted primarily of the programs operated by the Labor Market Board and can be divided into four main groups:

1. Employment and counseling services designed to shorten spells of unemployment.
2. Programs to improve the flow of labor, mainly through relocation and training allowances.
3. Programs designed to increase the demand for labor, including temporary employment, subsidies, and special measures for the handicapped.
4. Unemployment benefits.

For the fiscal year 1986/1987, 10 percent of labor market expenditures were allocated to the state employment service, 21 percent went for training, 38 percent went for labor supply programs, and 31 percent represented unemployment benefits of various kinds. An idea of the relative magnitude of the board's budget may be gained from the fact that it constituted more than 3 percent of the country's national product for the year.

While the employment offices are generally allotted only 10 percent of the budget, they have been of crucial importance in the overall scheme. Private employment agencies are illegal, and, while employers may fill vacancies by various means, vacancies must be reported to the public offices. About 600,000 vacancies are reported each year, although 400,000 more that are filled internally by firms need not be reported.

Workers who want to receive unemployment benefits must register with the employment service. They are assigned a case worker who decides upon the appropriate program to be followed and supervises their progress until they are reemployed. If they have an adequate vocational objective, either through experience or stated desire, they can be directed to job search authorities or to a training program. Otherwise they may be sent to an assessment center for testing and counseling before being assigned to a training program.

Training is the strongest element in the Swedish system. Approximately 1 percent of the entire adult labor force is enrolled in one of the programs each year. Most of the courses are given in special centers, but vocational schools and private employers may be involved where appropriate. Courses may last from a few weeks to several years, the latter offered in cooperation with the regular schools. The average course duration in a recent year was seventeen weeks. While in training, participants receive benefits equal to the unemployment benefits to which they may be entitled.

Follow-ups of trainees who completed their courses in 1986 revealed that 68 percent were employed in regular jobs six months later, most of them in the occupations for which they had been trained. About 18 percent of the trainees that year were handicapped, while another 18 percent were foreign nationals. In-house training can be arranged with private firms, primarily when designed to reduce skill bottlenecks, to cope with structural change, or to redress the sex balance in particular occupations. About 20 percent of training is given in this manner with the government bearing the cost.

The training programs have not been without their problems. There has been rigidity in the offerings, resulting in overproduction in some occupations—basic metal crafts and welding, for example—and an insufficient number of technicians and engineers. Neither employers nor the employment service has been sufficiently successful in forecasting skill requirements, which is essential if programs are to be adjusted in a flexible manner. However, training is offered for some 300 occupations, an impressive number given the absolute size of the program.

Efforts are made to simulate working environments rather than schoolrooms in the courses arranged by the Labor Market Boards. Industrial trainees punch time clocks to ensure regular attendance and may be penalized for excessive absenteeism. Instruction is individual or in small groups, with the instructor acting more like a plant supervisor than a teacher. Practice assignments are given in the form of job tickets and output is monitored for quality.

Because of the breadth of the Swedish system and its acceptance as an integral part of the labor market, there is none of the stigma that attaches, for example, to many American trainees, who are often drawn from groups that are hard to employ for one reason or another. Employers are not reluctant to hire the Swedish trainees, and the process of finding them appropriate jobs is facilitated by the presence of placement offices at the main training centers.

Occupationally handicapped workers constitute about 10 percent of the job seekers registered with the employment service. Those who are most severely handicapped are placed in sheltered workshops, while those who can hold down regular jobs are provided with wage subsidies. These start at 90 percent of the appropriate wage with a reduction to 25 percent in the course of a few years.

People between the ages of eighteen and twenty who cannot find jobs or a suitable training program are entitled to join a youth team within three weeks of reporting to the employment service. There they work an average of four hours a day in some form of public employment and receive counseling. In 1986/1987, the average length of stay in a youth team was six and one-half months. Half of those leaving obtained jobs while the rest left for other reasons or were placed on the job applicant roster. A recent program arranges the employment of youths in private firms, where they carry out regular duties at the going wage rates for up to six months. Many of them stay on with the same employer. As a result of these programs, youth unemployment is no longer a major problem.

Geographical relocation is another aspect of the active labor market policy. The compulsory reporting of vacancies to the employment offices, which provides them with a current listing of available jobs, facilitates the process. Relocation grants include travel expenses for unemployed workers as well as moving costs. Up to July 1987, starting subsidies were paid to cover the expenses of settling in, but these have been terminated. If all else fails, temporary public employment can be provided to bridge short-term spells of unemployment, and also to aid elderly, geographically immobile workers. These jobs cater primarily to women and youths.

None of this system could work without an adequately financed and competent administrative apparatus. Every municipality has an employment office that designates a contact officer for each local enterprise with more than fifty employees. This assures the offices of an in-depth knowledge of labor conditions within their jurisdictions. Special sections have been set up for workers in forestry, transportation, and construction, where the labor force is geographically mobile. Experimentation is urged upon the local offices.

At least two questions may be asked in evaluating the Swedish system: Does it accomplish its objectives and do the benefits exceed the costs? The unemployment statistics offer a positive answer to the first question. Even if an adjustment were made by counting trainees as unemployed, Swedish unemployment rates would be far below those of any country except Japan, whose recession rates should be increased to account for employees who are maintained on company payrolls with the help of government subsidies and who perform little if any productive work.

Low Swedish unemployment during the 1980s cannot be attributed to rapid economic growth or to the exceptional performance of industry. Swedish GNP growth during this decade was about average for our group of countries, while industrial output actually increased less rapidly than in Japan and the United States. Swedish manufacturing underwent a severe restructuring, as has already been noted, and lost 50,000 jobs in the process. There were large employment losses in shipbuilding, textiles, rubber, wood products, and iron and steel. These were offset in part by gains in the automobile and high technology industries. A recent study by the Brookings Institution concluded that "Sweden has been somewhat more successful than either the United States or Japan in moving out of basic industries—the employment share in basic industries has fallen relatively more in Sweden than in either the United States or Japan."[2] The Labor Market Board deserves credit for helping to accomplish this transition in an orderly fashion.

Cost is more difficult to evaluate. As noted earlier, Sweden has been devoting about 3 percent of its GNP to labor market programs, a massive expenditure by international standards. The Labor Market Board developed a cost/benefit model to help it allocate funds and made this observation: " 'Earnings' from placements are based on an estimate of their effects on government finance. For example, the net effect of employment training is the anticipated increase in tax revenue resulting from higher pay and shorter periods of unemployment, less training costs and benefits paid. The result was a 'deficit' in the administrative budget at the beginning of the 1980s, changing to a 'surplus' of more than 20 percent in recent years."[3]

This is not a fully satisfactory answer. On a more general level, what is involved is the collective objective function of the Swedish people. The elimination of unemployment remains a high-priority social goal. There are differences of opinion on particular aspects of the program, but there is no disposition to reduce the expenditures that are entailed.

The Swedish model is not for every country. Administration would be more complicated in larger nations. Differences in the composition of the labor force, the structure of employment, mobility patterns, and educational levels, as well as other factors, would add to the difficulties. But at least one lesson of the Swedish experience is clear: a pervasive and well-funded employment service is an essential ingredient in the development of a smoothly functioning labor market. Such a service can reduce to a minimum the inefficiencies resulting from the lack of information, counseling, and training of those unfortunate enough to lose their jobs through no fault of their own.

GREAT BRITAIN

Second only to Sweden in the use of direct labor markets intervention to reduce unemployment has been Great Britain, but it has shown neither the same degree of commitment to the attainment of full employment nor a political consensus of its desirability at all costs. The British Labor and Conservative parties have had different views on how to deal with unemployment. These differences are reflected in the mix of measures that have been tried.

At the center of British labor market management is the Manpower Services Commission, which came into being in 1974. It consists of representatives of organized labor and employers, as well as the national government and local government authorities. Regional commissions are similarly constituted. The commission operates through a network of more than a thousand job centers scattered throughout the country. Since the commission was created, more than twenty-five schemes have been designed to reduce unemployment. Most of them were of short duration and did not involve large numbers of people. The commission also has jurisdiction over labor market activities other than unemployment relief.

The various programs designed to alleviate unemployment can be divided into three broad categories:

1. *Public Employment Programs.* The largest of these is the Community Program, initiated in 1982 as a substitute for earlier Job Creation, Special Temporary Employment, and Community Enterprise programs. The purpose of the Community Program is to provide temporary work for up to one year for the long-term unemployed. Projects may be sponsored by local governments, private employers, or nonprofit institutions. The major conditions are that the work must be of genuine benefit to the community and that it does not replace projects that would have been undertaken in any event. Environmental improvement and the provision of social amenities are the most common types of work that are eligible.

Participants are paid the local rate for the job and are supposed to acquire additional skills and experiences that will help them find permanent employment. The 1986/1987 budget provided for 230,000 places, about 7 percent of the registered unemployed. Studies of the subsequent careers of earlier participants have suggested that this temporary work doubled their chances of finding regular jobs. This result is not too surprising since two-thirds of these participants were under twenty-five years of age and may have acquired better working habits. The principal criticism of the scheme is that it has not been large enough to meet the demand for participation. A much smaller Community Industry Program operates through charitable agencies and provides 7,000 positions for disadvantaged young people. Pay is also at local rates.

The Voluntary Projects Program differs from the others in that participants are not paid, although they may receive unemployment benefits. The theory is that they will be practicing existing skills and acquiring new ones that will enhance their opportunities in the open labor market. That the program has some appeal is evidenced by the fact that at the end of 1986, for example, 70,000 volunteers were participating in 350 projects.

The Conservative government that came into office in 1979 was of the view that the best way to combat unemployment was to remove obstacles to labor mobility in the private sector. It abolished or reduced some public employment programs, but mounting unemployment induced it to maintain the Community Program.

2. *Employment Subsidy Programs.* More to the liking of the Conservatives are several programs designed to stimulate entrepreneurial activities by unemployed people. The Enterprise Allowance scheme, which was launched in 1983, provides for the payment of a small weekly allowance for a maximum of fifty-two weeks to an unemployed person who establishes an enterprise. During 1985/1986, some 60,000 people received assistance under the scheme. The Manpower Commission claims that there has been a good survival rate for such enterprises and that many new jobs have been created. It is a condition of government assistance that recipients of government support invest at least £1,000 that has been obtained elsewhere.

Two new programs were initiated in 1986. The Jobstart Allowance derives from the theory that some of the unemployed may be discouraged by the low wages that they are offered during job searches. The government is prepared to pay them a wage supplement for six months to induce them to accept poorly paid jobs. The New Workers scheme involves a subsidy to employers who hire people under twenty-one years of age at rates of pay that are consonant with their experience. This has replaced the Young Workers scheme, which was criticized for leading to the displacement of older workers. There are safeguards to prevent this from happening under the new program.

A job-splitting scheme was introduced in 1983 in an effort to induce employers to create two or more part-time jobs to replace one full-time job. In this plan, the government subsidized employers to cover administrative and training costs. This has not been a success in terms of job creation.

3. *Training.* The Youth Training Scheme, which is designed to assist young people who have difficulty in finding employment when they leave school, is the largest program administered by the Manpower Services Commission. Sixteen-year-olds can receive two years of training, and seventeen-year-olds can receive one year. Young people

are offered a place within six months of leaving school, plus a weekly allowance while in training. About 400,000 entered the program in 1985/1986.

The Manpower Services Commission claims that this program has been very successful. A survey of graduates revealed that 57 percent of them were at work within three months, while another 9 percent were taking further training. There is no clear evidence, however, that the scheme has changed basic employability. Fewer young people than expected have been enrolling, perhaps because of the belief that high unemployment makes post-graduation jobs doubtful.

The Job Training Program is open to unemployed individuals over eighteen years of age. It consists of a number of sub-programs, the largest of which is the Job Training scheme. Under its auspices, intensive courses in a wide range of skills are offered, the largest being in clerical, computer, and automotive engineering trades. The Wider Opportunities Training program is aimed at people who want to broaden their skills. The National Priority Skills scheme offers training that may help increase the competitiveness of British industry. Training for Enterprise is designed to enhance the ability of people to start or expand small firms. These and other adult training programs attracted 55,000 people in 1985/1986.

In 1990, the government initiated a plan involving the creation of training and enterprise councils (TECs). These are local bodies with an average of fifteen directors, two-thirds of whom are to be top private-sector managers. The role of the TECs is to tailor training programs to local needs. They operate with government support. Most of the funds at their disposal are to come from the Youth Training scheme and from those intended to deal with the long-term unemployed. *The Economist* has observed that the TECs have been introduced into an already overcrowded world. "Even academic and civil servants who spend their lives studying or administering training programs complain that they cannot keep up with the range of organizations and the pace of change. . . . When the Thames Valley TEC conducted a survey of business awareness of government schemes, the second-highest score went to one that didn't even exist."[4]

In addition to these three major categories, there is a miscellany of other programs also aimed at improving the efficient operation of the labor market. Under the Restart Program, which commenced in 1986, all those who have been out of work for a year or more are invited to a Job Center for in-depth counseling; they may attend a special course set up to motivate them to seek employment or placement in the various schemes. Job Clubs offer sessions on how to look for work. The Job Release Scheme finances early retirement by providing workers with benefits, provided that their employer replaces the older workers with unemployed substitutes. The Manpower Commission also runs rehabilitation centers for the disabled and handicapped, a professional and executive recruitment service, and, of course, a general placement service. During 1985/1986, some 2.5 million vacancies were reported to the Job Centers, representing an estimated one-third of all vacancies that occurred during the period. Almost 2 million placements were made through the Job Centers.

When all these programs are added up, something on the order of 750,000 people were involved in 1985/1986, not including ordinary placements. There were 3.3 million unemployed in January 1986, which meant that about one-quarter of them had been assisted by Manpower Commission programs in one way or another. The commission's budget for that year was about 0.7 percent of the national product. However, this did not include unemployment benefits, which in the case of Sweden constitute about 30 percent of Labor Market Board expenditures. If the data for Sweden are adjusted accordingly, its comparable labor market expenditure falls to about 2 percent of the national product.

How effective has this panoply of British programs been in actually reducing unemployment, which ran at double-digit levels for seven of the ten years of the 1980s? An immediate reaction would be "not very," but the question remains whether unemployment would have been greater in the absence of government intervention. After all, France, Canada, and the Netherlands did just as badly as Britain during the same period. Among other things, Britain was more seriously affected by industrial restructuring than its major partners. Between 1980 and 1986, Britain lost 25 percent of its manufacturing jobs, a high figure in comparative terms.

In the view of one analyst, "efforts to improve employability appear to have made little net contribution to resolving unemployment. At best they seem to merely reshuffle the pack, inserting a marginal labor market candidate into work at the expense of a previous intra-marginal one."[5] This may be too harsh a judgment; another analyst reaches the conclusion that "the UK has, little by little, improved the range of training available from the public sector. . . . There is a very strong case for increasing further the training schemes on offer to young and not so young alike, as long as structural unemployment remains a key feature of the labor market."[6]

As the result of an expanding economy, Britain entered the 1990s with a much lower rate of unemployment than had prevailed during the previous decade. Nevertheless, the commitment to industrial training, which is supported by all shades of opinion, persists. The Labor Party is dedicated to improving the educational system and post-school remedial training. If it should regain power, expenditures on these programs as well as others designed to help the unemployed are likely to increase.

THE UNITED STATES

The United States has been less disposed than Britain to attempt to reduce unemployment through government intervention in the labor market. This does not mean that the federal and state governments have refrained from experiments with public employment, subsidies to private enterprises, and training. As far back as the 1930s, a bewildering series of programs has been tried, particularly when unemployment was high. But it is fair to say that there has never been a comprehensive, long-term policy. Rather, resources have often been devoted to poorly planned *ad hoc* programs.

A second deficiency lies in administration. The United States does not have a national employment service. Employment offices are operated by the individual states; there are about 2,600 of them, with wide variation in the quality of their performance. Their main task has been to dispense unemployment benefits. Employers have complained that they have concentrated on placing the poor and disadvantaged rather than on filling normal requirements. At the same time, employers have been reluctant to hire through the state employment offices. This creates a vicious circle, with the result that relatively few vacancies are filled in this manner.

Sharp differences in political attitudes toward labor market policy have been another obstacle to manpower programs. For example, the Reagan administration strongly opposed the whole concept of public jobs and put its trust in the private sector, whereas previous administrations had relied on a mixture of the two.

During the mid-1970s, when U.S. rates of unemployment were running above 8 percent, and again in the early 1980s, when they were almost 10 percent, Congress appropriated funds for manpower programs designed to bring the rates down. Interest waned as the decade progressed and unemployment fell back to politically acceptable levels, resulting in a mood of self-congratulation for having solved the most recent unemployment difficulties through market forces. From 1980 to 1988, employment in the United States increased by over 15 million persons, whereas few new jobs were added in Europe and less than 5 million in Japan. Contrary to the common European perception, the additional jobs, which were mainly in the service sector, paid on average as well as the manufacturing jobs that they had replaced. Had this employment surge not taken place, the United States would be in the midst of a devastating unemployment crisis.

The Comprehensive Employment and Training Act of 1973 (CETA)

This law is a good place to begin a review of U.S. labor market programs. The legislation consolidated a dozen small programs that had been in effect for some time. In its original form, it had three main components. The first consisted of grants of funds to state and local governments for training purposes, leaving those governments free to decide how the funds were to be spent. A second section provided for an initially small public service program to operate in areas where the rate of unemployment was over 6.5 percent. A third portion stipulated direct federal operation of programs aimed at particular groups including Indians, migratory workers, and young people.

Soon after CETA came into effect, the country experienced a recession as a result of the oil embargo. Unemployment rose rapidly. Congress reacted by expanding the public service portion of the law. Emphasis was placed on rapid hiring and, by 1978, 755,000 individuals were in the program. It was widely rumored that many of them were already in the employment of municipalities that were hard pressed financially and had simply substituted the new federal funds for their own payrolls. As a result, the act was amended, limiting eligibility to the socially disadvantaged and putting a stringent cap on wages and tenure. Enrollment began to fall, and the public service program came to an end in 1981. At that time, the incoming Reagan administration convinced Congress that a combination of high cost and payroll substitution warranted its termination.

The portion of CETA not devoted to public service went mainly for training, with the emphasis on young people. Training was done primarily in institutions rather than on the job, largely as a result of employer reluctance to accommodate the trainees.

CETA had mixed reviews for its economic effectiveness. For example, women did better than men in terms of post-training earnings. In fact, male participants appear to have benefited little if at all in this respect. On the other hand, the public service activities brought to local communities improved library services, road repair, record system modernization, and other marginal services that might not have been available without the federal funds. Where projects were administered well, which was by no means universal, young people received valuable work experience.

There is consensus that CETA helped to provide employment when the economy was slack. The net effect was small, lowering the rate of unemployment by an estimated 0.5 percent when the program was at its peak. Cost/benefit studies uniformly showed a program cost higher than subsequent wage benefits per participant. However, such intangibles as the value of useful work as an alternative to idleness—an important morale builder for many people—were not taken into account. CETA evaluations were done against the background of a depressed economy; it would be interesting to track the careers of CETA graduates after almost a decade of low unemployment.

The Job Training Partnership Act of 1982 (JTPA)

This legislation replaced CETA and marked a shift in labor market policy in accord with Republican Party views. Public service employment was terminated, the role of the federal government reduced, and administration turned over largely to the states and to private firms. The federal government retained only programs for Indians, migratory workers, and military veterans.

The philosophy of the act was apparent from its funding provisions. Block grants were made to the states with a minimum of guidance beyond the general purposes stated in the legislation. The states in turn distributed the funds to local jurisdictions, called service delivery areas (about 600 in the entire country). Funding averaged about $3.5 billion a year, which came to roughly 0.08 percent of the 1987 national product.

About 75 percent of the money was allocated to the states, the rest being administered by the federal government.

The act mandated the creation of a private industry council in each area. Membership of these councils averaged twenty-five, but they varied considerably in size. Members were appointed by local officials, and most were unpaid. At least 51 percent of the members were to represent business organizations, half from small firms. The rest were drawn from a variety of organizations, including trade unions and educational institutions. The function of these councils was to provide policy guidance and to oversee training activities.

The nature and purpose of the training programs provided was clear from data relating to their participants. Out of 753,000 enrolled in 1985, for example, 92 percent were economically disadvantaged, 53 percent were female, 42 percent were twenty-one years or younger, and 40 percent were receiving public financial assistance. Very few experienced older workers were involved.

Unlike CETA, regular stipends were not paid to trainees, although payments based on need and on the supportive services necessary to allow individuals to participate were permitted. This may have limited participation, although the evidence is mixed. People receiving other types of support were not eligible for payments except for such items as expenses and child care.

The types of training offered were determined by each service area, depending on local needs. Job training accounted for about 25 percent of the total, the rest being carried out in classrooms. In 1985, 657,000 participants completed courses averaging fourteen weeks each. Of these, 408,000 participants found jobs at the completion of their training, a good ratio considering the nature of the population involved.

The National Commission for Employment Policy, an independent agency established under the act to evaluate Job Partnership programs, among other things, reached the following conclusion after four years of experience:

Most observers agree that performance standards . . . have helped to establish the "image" of JTPA as an efficient, cost-effective program. Critics, however, charge that the standards have had an undesirable effect on client selection (leading to "creaming" of the most job-ready); the length (short) and content . . . of programs; and expenditure rates (below planned levels). On the other hand, results indicate that overall placement rates are high and that most

PIC [private industry council] chairs and SDA [service delivery area] directors who commented in a national survey are satisfied with program outcomes.[7]

Training programs were not the only ones financed under JTPA, although they were the most important, absorbing about three-quarters of the budget. The Dislocated Worker program, also administered by the states, provided assistance to individuals laid off from jobs to which they were unlikely to return and to long-term unemployed persons with poor prospects of future employment in their previous occupations. This program was aimed primarily at workers affected by industrial restructuring. Considering the magnitude of the problem, it was very small.

The federal government itself ran programs to help provide employment assistance to American Indians, a group with special problems. Another relatively minor program was designed to help migratory farm workers locate jobs. A Job Corps, modeled after a similar program that had proved very successful in the 1930s, provided economically disadvantaged young men and women with a maximum of one year of training in a residential setting. Funds were available for about 100,000 persons a year.

Annual expenditures of $3.5 billion a year for labor market programs may seem like a great deal of money, but they were relatively small compared with those of many other industrial nations. Although the unemployment rate was only 6.2 percent in 1987, for example, this figure represented approximately 7 million people who were looking for work and unable to find it, plus an indeterminate additional number who dropped out of the labor market because they did not think they could find work. It is true that many of the unemployed are in transition from one job to another, but some have been unemployed for long periods. Young people represent a particularly difficult problem. In 1988, when overall unemployment was 5.5 percent, the rate of employment for white males between sixteen and nineteen years of age was 13.9 percent, and for black males in the same age group, 32.7 percent. Youth unemployment has had particularly damaging social consequences.

The Job Training and Partnership Act was expanded by the Economic Dislocation and Worker Adjustment Assistance Act of 1988. The formula of providing block grants to states has been retained, but more emphasis has been placed on providing assistance to dislocated workers. Earlier legislation had been intended to assist the job search of workers whose employment had been lost because of imports, but it was gradually whittled down into an extension of unemployment benefits. The new legislation, it is hoped, will strengthen the programs for training and assisting dislocated workers, whether the cause of their displacement is foreign trade or business adversity. The emphasis will be on training and reemployment rather than the income support that characterized the previous programs.

There is a great deal of skepticism in the United States about the feasibility of government intervention in the labor market as a means of reducing unemployment. Past experience with CETA and Job Partnership have not increased public confidence in this approach. The programs that were put into effect under the umbrella of these two pieces of legislation often suffered from poor administration, in part because of the absence of a national employment service and the underfunding of state employment offices. These were too small to mount an effective attack on the problem. It is doubtful whether much more, if anything, will be done as long as unemployment remains relatively low. If it should increase once again to the levels that prevailed at the beginning of the 1980s, however, it might be a good investment for the country to consider adopting a more comprehensive system with stronger federal input to ensure better quality control.

GERMANY

Until the recession of 1974–1975, German economic growth was sufficiently rapid to take care of any labor market problems. The downturn that began at that time led to significant unemployment for the first time since the postwar reconstruction of the economy. The unemployment rate slowly declined during the next few years, but a renewal of recession in 1980 led to a rising level that reached a peak of 7.5 percent in 1985. Since then, there has been slow improvement, but unemployment has remained above the levels in the United States and Japan.

These figures are important for an understanding of German labor market policy. Germans have a particular reason for disliking unemployment. The extremely high level that characterized the later years of the Weimar period played a major role in the rise of the Nazis. The current rate is far from a level that might threaten the country's political stability, but it is troubling nonetheless.

The Employment Promotion Act of 1969 marked the beginning of modern labor market policy in Germany. Its original purpose was to provide further training for people who were already employed but wanted to improve their skills, in order to provide manpower for what was perceived as a long-term shortage of skilled personnel. In 1973, on the eve of the recession, only 4 percent of those enrolled in government-sponsored training courses had been unemployed at the time of entry. This and subsequent programs were directed by the Federal Employment Institute (FEI), which is also in charge of unemployment insurance. The FEI is headed by a tripartite board and funded by payroll taxes. It operates through a network of 500 employment offices.

Training and retraining are at the core of German policy. Until the mid-1970s, local employment offices issued training vouchers to those who qualified; these individuals then selected the programs in which they were interested. But when the focus shifted to the unemployed, the local offices began to play a more active role in placing them. Most of the training is now done outside FEI institutions, which handle only about 5 percent of the trainees. Public schools serve 20 percent, trade union schools 10 percent, and employer facilities the rest. Local offices often plan and design new courses that are then contracted out to the various training institutions. By the mid-1980s, two-thirds of those who entered training courses were registered as unemployed, showing how far the program had shifted from its original purpose.

It is important to note that as in Sweden, the local employment offices are crucial elements in the system. There are no private placement offices in Germany; only the FEI and its subsidiary bodies are authorized to provide such services. In 1986, the local offices effected more than 2 million placements and were the principal mechanism through which training course graduates found jobs. They have played a central role in matching course offerings with local needs.

Program costs have been controlled by adjusting eligibility standards and trainee stipends. Under the original act, anyone who was accepted for training could be paid up to 95 percent of previous earnings. The regulations were changed in 1976; unemployed individuals could receive 80 percent of previous wages, while all others received 58 percent. Stipends were reduced over the next decade. By 1986, only those for whom training was considered essential for successful working careers could receive stipends—up to 73 percent of previous wages—while those for whom further training was deemed "suitable" were eligible only for loans. There was an important exception, however; trainees eligible for unemployment benefits could receive stipends matching such compensation.

Despite these economies, the FEI training program is not a cheap one. There were over 400,000 participants in 1986, for example, and the budgetary allocation was more than $2 billion. Another $1.5 billion went for other unemployment relief programs (described below), the two totaling 0.4 percent of the national product. It will be recalled that the U.S. labor market program was funded at approximately the same absolute amount but at a smaller proportion of its GNP.

Germany has had access to a labor policy instrument that was not available to most other countries. The labor shortage of the 1960s was overcome in part by permitting foreigners to seek work in Germany. There were 2.6 million of these "guest workers" in the country in 1973, a number that was reduced by 700,000 during the subsequent recession. Unemployed foreign workers who had exhausted their unemployment benefits and had worked in Germany for less than five years could lose their work permits and were obliged to return to their native lands. Subsequently, however, this method of reducing unemployment pressures was no longer available since most of the "guest workers" had attained permanent resident status.

Although training has been the keystone of German unemployment policy, there have been other programs as well. The FEI started work creation schemes in the 1970s under the auspices of a Socialist-led government; these have continued under the Christian Democrats despite the lack of enthusiasm of the latter for this approach. These schemes resemble the American CETA program; projects must be in the public interest and are executed by public bodies or non-profit institutions. The FEI pays between 60 and 100 percent of the wages of those employed under these auspices.

These initiatives met many of the same criticisms that CETA faced. There is the problem of fiscal substitution by hard-pressed municipalities. There is also the question of whether this form of subsidized work has any effect on regular employment. Defenders of the program assert that the projects have a multiplier effect that adds an additional 50 percent of jobs to those created directly. Whatever the final balance, the Christian Democrats have been obliged to swallow their dislike of this approach because of rising unemployment. Budgetary support rose from DM 920 million in 1982 to DM 3 billion in 1986.

The FEI has also sponsored a wage subsidy program designed to find jobs for those who are hard to place by providing 80 percent of their wage costs for a period of six to twelve months. Employers have often been reluctant to hire those eligible for this assistance in a period of high unemployment, nor was there any guarantee that employment would be continued beyond the period of subsidy.

The Organization for Economic Cooperation and Development (OECD) conducted a cost/benefit analysis of the German employment programs as a whole for the year 1982, asking the following question: What would have been the cost of paying unemployment benefits to those who participated in the various manpower schemes? The budgeted program cost per person was DM 35,700 for the year, about DM 10,000 more than the cost of unemployment benefits. However, most trainees profited from having improved their qualifications after completing the courses. They earned higher incomes than in their previous employment, presumably reflecting increased productivity. For the job creation programs, the multiplier effect yielded additional revenues to the national budget. The OECD therefore reached the following conclusion:

The average number of registered unemployed would have been higher by some 200,000 to 300,000 persons but for these [labor market] activities. Consequently the expenditures on unemployment and the losses in revenues would have been much higher. From the point of view of the productive and future-oriented use of resources, more intensive recourse to these instruments would have been desirable to help the high and increasing number of unemployed.[8]

In sum, the German training program appears to offer good quality, useful instruction. Course completion is high, with drop-out rates of only about 20 percent. Post-training placement levels have been satisfactory. The German program has certainly not been as extensive as the Swedish one, but it has made a substantial contribution to the smooth working of the labor market.

Finally, mention should be made of a recent piece of legislation, the Employment Protection Act of 1985, which was designed to increase labor market flexibility without imposing any additional costs on the FEI. What this law does is to extend to eighteen months the maximum period of so-called short-term labor contracts, after which employers may lay off workers without severance pay or other formalities. Its intent is to induce employers to hire workers early in an economic upswing before it is certain that they will be needed permanently. It is not yet clear whether the purpose of the law has been realized in practice.

FRANCE

France has had a high rate of unemployment during most of the 1980s, reaching a maximum of 10.8 percent in 1987. Successive governments have attempted to mitigate its impact through a variety of labor market programs. There has been little in the way of a central theme or consistency in their approaches. *Ad hoc* measures have been adopted to deal with immediate problems. Analysts have remarked that the "combination of innovations and continuity, the juxtaposition of contradictory measures, and changes of intention make real change difficult to identify."9

Easing restrictions on layoffs to make the labor market more flexible was considered in the previous chapter, and opening jobs through early retirement and reduced working hours will be dealt with in the next chapter. Other types of labor market intervention, some of them quite imaginative if not always effective, will be surveyed here.

The government agency responsible for administering the programs is the National Employment Agency, established in 1967. Its original task was to supervise the placement work of local offices, but its mandate was later broadened to include training and other activities. As in the case of Germany, the initial French reaction to rising unemployment was to reduce the number of foreign workers. Immigration was suspended in 1974. A few years later, foreign workers who agreed to leave the country were made eligible for lump sum payments. Because many of the foreigners were Algerians whose prospects for finding jobs at home were poor, there were relatively few takers.

An innovative program introduced in 1980 allowed newly unemployed workers to take up to a year's unemployment entitlement in a lump sum payment for the purpose of starting a new business. If additional jobs were created in the process, the payment could be increased. The program proved popular; by the end of 1984, 170,000 people had applied for payments. The government estimated that between 30 and 40 percent of all new firms started during a two-year period resulted from these payments, and that about 70 percent of them survived for at least three years. How cost effective the scheme has been is another matter; that calculation would depend in part on the value of the unemployment benefit offset as well as the profitability of the new firms.

Youth training and employment programs have absorbed more employment agency funds than any of thé others. "Youth employment pacts" were introduced in 1977; these exempted employers who hired persons under twenty-five years of age from paying social security taxes for them until they reached twenty-five. The pacts had two conditions: There had to be a minimum employment period of six months and there could be no decrease in the labor force while a pact was in effect. The Youth Future Plan came into effect in 1982, providing special training to facilitate entry into work for the underprivileged. Still another program subsidized employers for each hour of work made available for training in a combined work and training schedule.

These and other youth schemes have been criticized for their temporary character and fluctuating support. Studies have indicated that only 20 percent of trainees between ages sixteen and eighteen received certificates of competency, and only 36 percent of them secured regular jobs after completing their training. Nevertheless, the programs did make a dent in unemployment. By 1986, there were 400,000 participants in the various schemes, half employed on community contracts. The fact that a majority of the trainees were not counted as unemployed reduced the rate of unemployment by more than 1 percent.

There have also been training programs for adults but they have not been as extensive as those for young people. Continuous or further training is financed both by the state and by employers, who are required to spend at least 1.1 percent of their payrolls for this purpose.

The changing emphasis of French labor market policy emerges from financial data. Unemployment benefits accounted for 40.8 percent of total labor market expenditures in 1980, when the unemployment rate was 6.4 percent. By 1985, despite the fact that unemployment had reached 10.4 percent, the share of unemployment benefits had fallen to 34.1 percent. The rest consisted of incentive payments to induce people (older workers in particular) to withdraw from the labor market and training costs. Of this remainder, training absorbed 35 percent, job creation through lump sum payments 7 percent, and labor force reductions the balance. A respectable amount of money was spent on these programs: 0.8 percent of the GNP for training, 1.2 percent for the stimulation of labor force reduction, and 0.4 percent for other purposes.[10]

Despite these efforts, French unemployment has remained unsatisfactorily high. What the French experience suggests is that while active labor market measures can alleviate economic hardship and contribute to the formation of human capital, they cannot solve the underlying problems that give rise to the unemployment. Improving the efficiency of the labor market helps, but that is not enough.

JAPAN

The performance of the Japanese labor market is one of the most satisfactory of all the OECD countries. Unemployment during the 1980s has not exceeded 3 percent. Even if the rates are adjusted upward to reflect the practice of carrying redundant employees on payrolls, they would still be less than for the rest of the countries except Sweden, whose rates would also have to be raised because of the way in which unemployment is measured under its active labor market policy.

One of the consequences of the Japanese employment system is that there is a strong demand for young workers, so that youth unemployment is not a special problem. While there is a good deal of job changing among the young, the special measures common in other countries are not necessary in Japan. The main problem group consists of older people who have retired early. While the average age of the Japanese population is low, a combination of declining birth rates and increasing longevity is making for a rapidly aging labor force.

The Ministry of Labor is in charge of Japanese labor market policy. It operates through 500 employment offices that handle about a fifth of all job vacancies. Fee-charging private agencies are generally illegal except that they are permitted to place some categories of temporary workers. The ministry runs a variety of training programs open to both young and adult workers, but in fact most vocational training is done on the job, which is the avenue for employment with desirable firms.

The preferred instrument for labor market intervention is the subsidy. These are available to firms in depressed areas to enable them to employ displaced workers. In addition, a temporary transfer subsidy can provide financial support for firms that are moving employees to another enterprise with the expectation that they will come back; the state bears half the expenses involved. Half the salaries of employees who are hired directly from unemployment rolls can be subsidized for a period of three months. There are also regional subsidies to induce employers to move to depressed areas, seasonal subsidies to employers who maintain workers on their payrolls for specified periods during the low season, and special support for the handicapped.[11]

To facilitate the restructuring of Japanese industry, particularly steel and shipbuilding, the Ministry of Labor initiated a program in 1987 for 300,000 displaced workers. It was intended to encourage labor mobility through training and the transfer of personnel within and between companies, as well as to further regional employment growth. Almost 1,600 billion yen, amounting to 0.5 percent of the GNP, was appropriated for the program.[12] This was an unusual event. It demonstrated that when faced with the threat of rising unemployment, the Japanese government was prepared to move quickly, through subsidies to the private sector, to preserve the fiction of full employment.

NOTES

1. Gosta Rehn, "Swedish Active Labor Market Policy," *Industrial Relations* 24 (1985), p. 52.

2. Barry Bosworth and Alice M. Rivlin, eds., *The Swedish Economy* (Washington: Brookings Institution, 1987), p. 77.

3. *The Swedish Labor Market 1986/87*, Annual Report of the Swedish Labor Market Administration, Stockholm, 1987, p. 15.

4. *The Economist*, April 21–27, 1990, p. 64.

5. Rodney Stares, "The Management of the U.K. Labor Market, 1973–1983." In Howard Rosen, ed., *Comparative Labor Market Policies* (Washington: National Council on Employment Policy, 1986), p. 88.

6. Graham Todd, *Job Creation in the U.K.* (London: Economist Publications, 1986), pp. 81–82.

7. National Commission for Employment Policy, *The Job Training Partnership Act* (Washington: GPO, 1987), p. 81.

8. Organization for Economic Cooperation and Development (OECD), *A Challenge for Income Support Policies* (Paris: OECD, 1984), p. 166.

9. Marie Françoise Mouriaux and René Mouriaux, "Unemployment Policy in France, 1976–82." In Jeremy Richardson and Roger Henning, eds., *Unemployment* (London: Sage Publications, 1984), p. 164.

10. OECD, *Economic Surveys: France* (Paris: OECD, 1986/87), p. 37.

11. These programs are set out in detail in *Marginal Employment Subsidies* (Paris: OECD, 1982), pp. 59–70.

12. Japan Institute of Labor, *Japan Labor Bulletin* (March 1987), p. 4.

Chapter Six

WORKING TIME

During the past quarter of a century, major changes in the pattern of working time have occurred. These can be attributed to several factors: attempts by governments and private firms to reduce unemployment; the great increase in the rate of female labor force participation; the shift of employment from manufacturing to services; demographic changes reflected in the rising average age of the labor force; and an increased preference for leisure over work. The traditional standard work week is beginning to fade as more and more people are employed on alternative schedules, either by choice or necessity.

Working time can be measured in various units—hours, weeks, months, or years. All of these enter into the new schemes that are now proliferating. These schemes have broad similarities among them, due in part to international borrowing, but there is an almost endless variety of experiments and actual applications. They reflect the ability of the labor market to adjust to new requirements, often in the interest of greater efficiency of employment.

This subject has not attracted as much attention from economists as have the more familiar areas such as compensation, unemployment, trade union effects, and wage-price relationships, although there have been some honorable exceptions.[1] Yet working time is a fundamental aspect of working life. It is often as important to employee welfare and productive efficiency as other conditions of labor. There is a growing realization of its importance, and both governments and private firms have begun to allocate substantial resources to the investigation and promotion of new forms.

This chapter deals with some of the most interesting of the new working time patterns. It does not include the more familiar aspects of working time that have been developed over many years: the standard workweek, shift work, overtime, and weekend hours; nor does it offer comprehensive coverage of all the countries, which would require a book in itself.

PART-TIME WORK

There is no generally accepted definition of part-time work. The U.S. Bureau of Labor Statistics defines those who work less than thirty-five hours a week as partially employed. Japan also follows this practice. Sweden uses a cutoff point of thirty-six hours, while France and Britain use thirty hours. The International Labor Office defines part-time work as "any professional activity undertaken on a regular and voluntary basis for a certain number of hours per day or per week totalling a number of hours significantly below the normal working week," but it cites no specific norms.

To compound the problem of making international comparisons, the Bureau of Labor Statistics (BLS) includes seasonal and casual part-timers within the part-time rubric, while other countries count only those who are employed part-time on a regular basis. The European Community, in its labor force surveys, leaves the decision of their status to employees when they are polled.

OECD estimates the percentage of the labor force working part-time in recent years as follows:

	1979	1986
France	8.2	11.7
Germany	11.2	12.3
Japan	9.9	11.7
Sweden	23.6	23.5
United Kingdom	16.4	21.2
United States	16.4	17.4

Source: *OECD in Figures* (1988), pp. 14–15.

It may be noted that the BLS figure for the United States for 1986, including both voluntary and involuntary part-timers, was 17.8 percent, close to the OECD figure. Sweden and Britain stand out as particularly high in part-time work. Some of the reasons for this fact will appear in the discussion that follows.

Who Are the Part-Time Employed?

The first thing that can be said is that most of them are women. The following data for 1986 make this clear:

	Female part-time employment as a % of total female employment	Male part-time employment as a % of total male employment	Female part-time employment as a % of total part-time employment
France	23.1	3.5	83.0
Germany	28.4	2.1	89.8
Japan	22.8	5.5	70.0
Sweden	42.8	6.0	86.6
United Kingdom	44.9	4.2	88.5
United States	26.4	10.2	66.5

Source: *OECD in Figures* (1988), pp. 14–15.

A 1988 survey conducted by Japanese trade unions found that 32.6 percent of women workers worked part-time in that country, about a third of them employed under conditions that violated the labor standards law.[2] In the United States, about 60 percent of the women employed part-time were married, with their spouses present. In Britain (1981), 80 percent of women working part-time were married, compared with only half of the women working full-time.[3] A substantial proportion of the men who work part-time are either young or old.

Another characteristic of part-time employment is its concentration in the service sector. In the United States (1989), 34 percent of all who worked part-time were in the retail trade, with another 45 percent in other services. The proportion was not as large in Japan, where 45 percent were in trade but only 17 percent in other services (1986).

The incidence of part-time work for the labor force as a whole is partly a function of female labor force participation rates, which were as follows in 1986:

	Percent
France	55.3
Germany	50.4
Japan	57.4
Sweden	78.3
United Kingdom	61.0
United States	64.9

Source: OECD in Figures (1988), pp. 10–11.

A comparison of these figures with the data cited above on the part-time employment rates reveals a rough relationship between the two sets. The case of Sweden is particularly striking. It stands out both with respect to its female participation rate and the incidence of part-time work. Why so many Swedish women are working is a story that cannot be developed here. Suffice it to say that from 1979 to 1986, the net increase in the female labor force was greater than the net increase in the total labor force. If Swedish women had not entered the job market in increasing numbers, the total labor force would have declined.

Another characteristic of part-time workers is their relatively low pay. The ratio of median hourly earnings of part to full time workers in the United States was 61.7 percent in 1989. However, it is likely that a substantial proportion of the differential is due to the preponderantly female composition of the part-time labor force and to the fact that many women are employed in low wage industries. It is probably true that the hourly wage of, say, women part-time cleaners is not much different from that of similarly employed full-timers. An interesting finding for the United States is that the median earnings for part-time women workers was higher than those for men in 1989 ($4.92 versus $4.62 per hour). This probably reflects the heavy representation of young and older workers among the men.[4]

Why Part-Time Work?

From 1979 to 1986, the proportion of part-time work increased in every country except for Sweden, which was already heavily engaged in this practice in 1979. Some of the increase may have been due to the onset of economic recession in 1981, but this should have been corrected during the subsequent upswing.

The more likely explanation is that there has been a secular increase in both the demand for and the supply of part-time employees. The growth of service employment has been a major factor on the demand side. In some of the expanding industries, part-time workers have offered a distinct advantage to employers. Many part-timers are not covered by such fringe benefits as health insurance and pension plans, and they are often entitled to shorter holidays. In the United States, for example, only about a third of part-time employees are covered by company-sponsored health plans, while the pension coverage is less than 30 percent for those working under 1,000 hours a year. In Japan, many part-time employees receive neither the overtime pay nor the vacations to which they are legally entitled.[5]

On the other side of the ledger is the possibility that some part-time employees may be entitled to full fringe benefits, leading to expensive fixed costs. If social security taxes are levied on only a portion of wages, the cost to the employer may be the same for part- and full-time employees, depending on the wage level. It may be difficult to provide health insurance on less than a full-time basis. The extent to which fixed minimum charges discourage part-time hiring depends largely on the legislative and collective agreement provisions in each country.

Perhaps the most significant benefit of part-time work to employers is the flexibility that it affords. This is particularly true in retailing, where there may be peaks of sales activity alternating with slow periods. Part-time employment may produce a significant reduction in labor costs. Still, there may be an offset factor in the cost of training and the provision of additional cooperating equipment. Moreover, there is no conclusive evidence that hourly productivity is higher for part-time employees to offset the greater training and capital expenses.[6]

On the labor supply side, much of the demand for part-time work comes from women who are trying to balance paid employment with domestic obligations, particularly child care. About three-quarters of all women working part-time in the United States in 1987 were doing so voluntarily, not because they could not find full-time employment. Not all of these were housewives, however. Some people who can afford it may prefer leisure to work. Younger people, men and women alike, may be attending school and need work to support themselves. Part-time work may also be a means of easing people into retirement, or it may be necessary for health reasons.

Part-time work does entail some disadvantages, apart from the lower level of earnings. Fringe benefits may not be available, as already noted. The jobs that are available tend to be concentrated at the lower end of the labor market and have poor career prospects. Even when the positions are good ones, as in the case of professionals, part-timers may be seen as not fully devoted to their work and less deserving of promotion. Self-employed individuals often fear to cut down their work loads lest additional patronage dry up. They physician who wants to reduce his working hours and turns patients away may find his referrals decreasing.

Trade unions are generally not enamored of the part-time option. They point out that part-timers tend to have fewer rights and less employment stability; they argue that much part-time work tends to be monotonous and repetitive. They deny that it has contributed to lower unemployment and much prefer the alternative of a general reduction of working hours. What they do not stress is the greater difficulty of organizing workers and retaining those on part-time as members. In Japan, with a global unionization rate of about 27 percent, only 6 percent of part-time employees are union members. In fact, most of the enterprise unions that dominate the scene in Japan admit only full-time regular workers to membership.[7]

Government Policy

Governments have generally looked favorably on part-time employment, motivated largely by the belief that it helps to alleviate unemployment. There is no evidence that this has occurred. The jobs that have disappeared due to industrial restructuring have affected mainly men engaged in manufacturing occupations. The increased demand for female labor has come from the expanding service sector.

The role of governments has been confined primarily to adapting labor legislation to the requirements of part-time employment. They have had to walk a fine line between measures designed to remove employer disincentives and those that raise employee receptivity. Social insurance and other mandatory programs pose particular problems.

The relevant legislative modifications differ among countries. A few examples illustrate the problems. In France, a number of employer payments, including local taxes, accident insurance premiums, and contributions to training programs, were levied in direct proportion to the number of employees, regardless of their hours. A law enacted in 1981 stipulated that, in determining the number of employees involved for tax purposes, part-time workers would be counted in proportion to the number of hours worked.

The problem of social insurance coverage may be illustrated by American conditions. Employers are taxed on the first $51,300 of pay for each employee at the present writing, regardless of hours worked. Thus, if there were two part-time employees each earning $35,000, the tax would be substantially greater than for one employee earning $70,000.

Some countries exempt employers from such taxes altogether for employees working below a specified minimum number of hours. A French employer can receive a tax rebate if he can demonstrate that two part-timers, each working between twenty and thirty hours a week, cost him more than what he would have had to pay for a single worker doing the same job. British workers employed for fewer than eight hours a week are not covered by many protective programs, but they are covered if they work from eight to sixteen hours after five years of continuous service. They receive full coverage over sixteen hours a week. The result of these exclusions, among other things, is that maternity and redundancy benefits are not received by an estimated 1 million part-time workers.

An experiment in the Netherlands deserves mention. Employers in several depressed areas there received subsidies for each part-time job created or for existing full-time jobs converted to part-time. Employees who made the switch received subsidies equal to 60 percent of the earnings foregone for the first six months and 30 percent for the next six months. Most of those affected were married women under thirty years of age who wanted more time for family life and who might have gone on part-time in any event. It should also be added that many in the Netherlands, which has suffered heavy unemployment, are true believers in the efficacy of work sharing as a cure.

In sum, the growth of part-time work is a response to an economic need on both sides of the labor market. It is generally popular among those engaged in it. To the extent that it permits women who could not otherwise accept paid employment to enter the mainstream of production, part-time work adds to the pool of labor available to the economy. To quote an OECD study, "part-time work provides a mechanism for effecting substantial reductions in working time without any offsetting increase, in any major sense, in labor costs." To facilitate it, what is required is "an accommodating tendency by suppliers of labor to fill part-time work places. The key here is the concept of the family unit as a supplier of labor, and the predominant growth of married female part timers gives reason to believe that further increases in this sort of labor supply are possible."[8]

JOB SHARING

This practice is often identified with part-time work. It is that, but something more as well. Job sharing involves the formal division of one job into two (or more) parts, each held by a different person. An employer may find that a part-time worker is all he or she needs to perform a specific task, but a job-sharing arrangement is feasible only when the task involved requires a full-time number of hours to complete. It is a more difficult arrangement to make, since it is necessary to find two individuals with similar skills, each of whom is prepared to work less than full-time.

The idea originated in the United States, largely because of the rapid growth of the female labor force. Its pioneers were primarily professional women who wanted to use their skills in the job market while simultaneously fulfilling their domestic obligations. Although clerical employees have become the largest group of job-sharers, there is a strong representation among professional, technical, and supervisory employees. A 1985 survey revealed that 11 percent of American employers had job-sharing programs, most of them less than five years old. The largest users were employers in health care (where there has been an endemic shortage of nurses), education, government, finance, insurance, and real estate.[9]

The scheme was slower to catch on in Europe. The British government in 1985 encouraged civil service departments to offer job sharing, and both local authorities and nonprofit organizations have done so. Many occupations are involved, ranging from physicians to probation officers to dry-cleaning employees, but the total number remains small.[10]

The German chemical industry began a job-sharing model in which a sharer was discharged automatically if his or her twin quit. Legislation was enacted in 1985 to protect sharers from this fate, but the practice is not widespread in Germany. In France, Mitterand advocated job sharing during his successful campaign for the French presidency in 1981, but a survey four years later, although admittedly incomplete, turned up only fifty job sharers in five firms. The practice appears to be more popular in Sweden, where 35 percent of the firms queried replied that they had made use of it.[11]

WHY JOB SHARING?

The impetus for job sharing came from employees, primarily from married women averaging 35 years of age who had young children. Some men have joined in, but in smaller numbers, because they are considered more career-oriented and less responsible for tasks at home. Sharing is sometimes used as a means of transition to retirement, but the fact that many pension plans base retirement benefits on the last few years of earnings inhibits it.

Job sharing has advantages and disadvantages for both employers and employees. On the plus side, it offers a means of retaining the services of skilled employees, particularly in periods of labor shortage. A substantial employer investment in training heightens the desirability of retaining employees. Absenteeism among sharers tends to be reduced because this system affords employees more time to carry out necessary chores and because job sharers are reluctant to place additional burdens on their partners. Labor turnover may be reduced, since the difficulty of arranging share jobs may induce sharers to stay with an accommodating employer. There is no evidence that job sharers are less productive than full-timers. Indeed, many have an incentive to perform well, since they hope eventually to secure full-time status with the same employer.

On the negative side, there may be fixed costs for fringe benefits, plus additional costs for administration and supervision. For employees, sharing a job might deprive them of the satisfaction of controlling its performance, which could be particularly important in professional work. Also, it is not unknown for friction to develop between the job sharers and thus disturb the relationship.

A number of factors have hindered the spread of job sharing. Management inertia is one. Unless an enterprise is forced to do so by labor market pressures, why depart from existing practice? Managers appear to be particularly opposed to the sharing of high-level jobs where it works best. Trade unions have been cool to the idea for many of the same reasons that lead them to oppose part-time work: the threat to full-time jobs and to reductions in the standard work week; the risk of employee exploitation; and the increased difficulty of recruiting union members. In the United States, however, several unions have negotiated agreements designed to protect job sharers. Unexpected opposition has arisen from feminist organizations, which fear that job sharing will tend to segregate women into less favorable portions of the labor market and to reinforce the stereotype of women as primarily homemakers.

It is difficult to predict the future of job sharing. There is a demand for it, but whether an adequate supply of appropriate jobs will become available depends largely on the state of the labor market for particular occupations. The limited experience to date suggests that job sharing is cost efficient in particular situations for which it is well suited: for highly motivated people who want to combine careers and raising families without a break in their service, not only for financial reasons but also because they are reluctant to abandon skills acquired at considerable cost and effort. A proponent of this approach summarizes its desirability as follows:

wherever job sharing has managed to make an appearance it turns out to be a remarkably positive work/life solution for those involved, and that is the point to stress in conclusion—it is a solution. It cannot meet the needs of everyone, or even of everyone who wants to work shorter hours, but it is one option that should at least be studied, to see if it should be made available for those who want it, because it can be highly successful and is evidently strongly desired by some—"evidently" because, they have had to overcome such odds to achieve it.[12]

RETIREMENT

The retirement age is a major determinant of the number of years that an individual devotes to working life. The average age of retirement varies considerably among countries as well as within countries over time. Increasing longevity is a significant factor in the extension of working life. When enterprises are under economic pressure to reduce staff, however, early retirement is often a favored solution.

Comparative international data on the age of retirement are hard to come by. There are good data for Japan, perhaps because retirement has been a controversial issue there. Until the 1980s, the large firms that practiced lifetime commitment usually required retirement at age fifty-five. This age has been rising, partly under government pressure and partly because both public and private pensions are inadequate. In 1987, 85 percent of firms with 5,000 or more employees had raised the retirement age to sixty, and a majority of firms of all sizes had reached this level. Very few, 5 percent of all firms, permitted employees to stay on beyond sixty.[13]

Until recently, the statutory or customary retirement age in most European countries was sixty-five for men and sixty for women. Early retirement schemes may have lowered the average, but governments and employers have opposed general reductions. The United States is the only country that does not permit mandatory retirement at any age, with minor exceptions; this has been enforced by federal legislation enacted after intense lobbying by organizations of older people. However, sixty-five remains the age at which retirees are eligible for full government pensions, while a majority of men are out of the labor force at about age sixty-two, when they can receive somewhat reduced pensions.

Partial Retirement

Sweden adopted a partial pension plan in 1975 and amended it in 1981. An employee between the ages of sixty and sixty-four, who reduces his or her working hours by at least five a week but still averages a minimum of seventeen hours, may be eligible for a special pension amounting to 50 percent of the resultant loss of earnings. The replacement rate had been 65 percent prior to 1981, but the popularity of the program and its cost led to the reduction. This does not alter the normal pension entitlement at age sixty-five, which is quite generous. In the first year after the plan came into operation, 12 percent of all those eligible applied for partial pensions. The number rose to 27 percent by 1980, but the reduction in the compensation rate has apparently diminished interest in the plan; by 1986, only 12 percent of those eligible were on partial pension.[14]

The modal reduction for partial retirees is to twenty hours per week, but many people, particularly women, opt for a shorter week. Employers are not obliged to consent to requests for part-time, but in practice most of them have agreed to it. During the recession of the early 1980s, many employers may have encouraged early retirement, but the subsequent drop in pension applicants may reflect a growing manpower shortage.

Early Retirement with a Replacement Condition

Sweden is unique in not requiring the employer to hire additional employees as a condition for the retirement subsidy.[15] Britain, France, and Germany have adopted schemes that are subject to this condition, the purpose of which is to increase employment opportunities for younger people. The British scheme became effective in 1976, the French in 1981, and the German in 1984. Consent of employers is necessary in all three countries, since it is their responsibility to find replacements. The general rule is that early retirement may take place up to five years before the normal pensionable age, and there are minimum years of service requirements.

In France, the program is activated only if the employer enters into a "solidarity contract" with the Ministry of Labor. As of 1985, about one-third of insured employees were with firms that had signed such contracts. Germany has a similar requirement, and the coverage appears to be about the same as the French. Britain does not require prior agreement.

The British scheme pays a specified rate of benefits, depending on the age at retirement and the income of the spouse if the retiree is married. The benefit amounts to 65 percent of prior earnings in France and Germany. The French and British schemes do not permit the early retirees to work, but in Germany they may do so for less than fifteen hours a week with a specified maximum amount of earnings.

Replacement is obligatory in Britain and France. It is voluntary in Germany; if the employer leaves the job vacant, however, he must bear the full cost of the pension and does not receive the partial 35 percent reimbursement from the government that is payable if he fills the job. In the other countries, the entire pension cost is borne by the government.

The German and British schemes require that replacements be drawn from unemployment rolls, while this is recommended but not obligatory in France. To prevent the plans from being used to accomplish normal manpower adjustments, a clear link must be shown between the job of the retiree and the replacement in Britain and Germany; the French police the system by requiring only that the firm's level of employment may not fall as a result of the retirement. In Germany and France, the replacements must be retained for two and one years respectively, while

Britain merely requires that the replacements receive indefinite tenure.

How attractive have these schemes been? The French take-up rate is high; an estimate puts the ratio of early retirees to the population aged fifty-five to sixty-four years at 11.7 percent. The British figure is much lower, only 3.4 percent in 1984. Preliminary estimates suggest that the German rate is substantially higher than the British.[16]

In Britain, a large majority of the applicants have been men, with a heavy weighting of unskilled and semi-skilled workers, as might be expected. The French scheme, however, has attracted mainly white-collar personnel, with only 20 percent coming from the ranks of blue-collar employees. This may have been because the French system ties the pension closely to previous earnings, which has discouraged low wage earners from applying.

The replacement rates vary from 95 percent in France, to 70-75 percent in Britain, and 60 percent in Germany. The French data are suspect, however, because of the loose manner in which replacements are determined. The British and German rates are more credible because the replacement obligation is more closely monitored.

How effective these programs have been in reducing unemployment can only be a matter of speculation. There are no data directly linking early retirement to the rate of unemployment. With respect to cost, French data for 1982 and 1983 suggest that the net cost of retiring a worker early varied between 50 to 75 percent more than the cost of maintaining an unemployed person on the various support schemes that are available. The comparable British figure was 10 percent. Why the British scheme should have been so much more cost efficient than the French can be determined only by a close comparative analysis of the two systems.

Because of the early standard retirement age that prevails in Japan, a negligible proportion of manufacturing companies that have had to make employment adjustments resorted to earlier retirement.[17] The Japanese tendency has been to move in the opposite direction, since the rapidly aging population and the growing demand for adequate pensions will put a severe financial strain on corporate and government pension systems. Legislation enacted in 1986 actually provides a government subsidy for firms with a work force of which more than 6 percent is aged sixty to sixty-five. The subsidy is payable for each employee above the 6 percent level. Plans are being made gradually to raise the public pensionable age from the current sixty years to sixty-five.

There have not been any recent substantial age modifications of the national pension in the United States. Retirement pensions have been available below the age of sixty-five for many years, but at the cost of lower future benefits. Private pensions are more widespread in the United States than in most other countries. A 1983 survey indicated that 58 percent of workers in larger firms were covered by plans that permitted early retirement, although they often entailed penalties. From 1970 to 1984, the labor force participation rate for workers in the sixty to sixty-four age group declined considerably less in the U.S. than it did in the four European countries studied. There are a number of possible reasons for this, including differences in unemployment rates and in the generosity of pension schemes, but the unavailability of preferential early retirement options may have been a factor as well.

An evaluation of twelve European countries with early retirement schemes similar to those described above came to the following conclusion:

From a long-term perspective, the advisability of encouraging premature retirement seems highly questionable. Given falling birth rates and subsequent future contractions in the working age population, labor force growth will come to a virtual standstill by the turn of the century. In addition, the ratio of pensioners to wage earners contributing to social security programs will rise. A more appropriate future policy would thus appear to call for gradually raising the mandatory age of retirement, while eliminating the incentive to early retirement.[18]

This may be too drastic a recommendation. Some jobs adversely affect the well-being of individuals without impairing their physical or mental capacities sufficiently to qualify them for disability benefits. A partial retirement system modeled on that of Sweden, for example, might be a reasonable option for countries that are able to afford it. As many retirees have learned to their sorrow, a sudden transition from full-time work to complete retirement may have traumatic effects. Difficult though it may be to include this factor in a cost/benefit analysis, it should be given some weight.

SHORT-TIME WORK

This can be defined as a reduction of working hours designed to avoid temporary layoffs. It differs from part-time work and job sharing in that it is not intended to be permanent, but rather to continue only until business picks up again. The motivation is solely to alleviate unemployment, not to accommodate employee convenience. Since staff rearrangements are likely to be more costly than partial layoffs, it has usually been necessary to subsidize enterprises to undertake the spreading of work. This has been the general practice in Europe and Japan, with only the United States holding back.

Britain has resorted extensively to such programs. A Temporary Employment Subsidy scheme was introduced in 1975, and, over a period of three-and-a-half years, 540,000 jobs were subsidized. The scheme was criticized on the ground that it was helping to maintain non-viable jobs that should have been terminated, so a more restrictive Temporary Short Time Working Compensation plan replaced it in 1979. The amount and duration of the subsidies was gradually reduced as time went on. During the first two years of the latter plan's operation, almost 720,000 employees were subsidized, but by 1983, the last full year before the scheme was terminated, the number had fallen to 142,000.[19]

Even opponents of the scheme acknowledged that it had some advantages. It enabled a firm to hold its labor force together in slumps of short duration, which was particularly important for skilled workers who might find other jobs. Negative views prevailed, however, the predominant fear being that the scheme delayed necessary industrial restructuring.

Short-time work subsidies are of long standing in Germany. There an enterprise, with the cooperation of its works council, must demonstrate that the shortage of work is unavoidable and that the only alternative to work sharing is dismissals. The short-time proposal must involve a reduction of at least 10 percent of total working time for a minimum of one-third of the labor force for at least four weeks. If these conditions are met, employees are eligible to receive allowances equal to 68 percent of their lost earnings. These payments, plus additional employer contributions, have meant that many people on short-time receive more than 90 percent of their previous earnings. The normal duration of payments is six months, but for some industries particularly hard hit by unemployment, it has been extended to as long as two years.

The number of workers on subsidy has varied with the business cycle. In 1978, when the rate of unemployment was down to 3.7 percent, subsidies were paid to 191,000 workers. By 1983, when unemployment had risen to 9.1 percent, more than 1 million workers were on short-term subsidies, and the number continued high for the next three years.

This is an expensive program and its cost effectiveness has been questioned. Would it not be better policy for firms to even out cyclical fluctuations by producing for inventory rather than by layoffs? Is short-time subsequently made up by overtime so that lost earnings are recovered in the normal course of business? The counter argument is that short-time work may be less expensive than regular employment compensation and that firms can thus avoid hiring and retraining costs. Whatever the validity of the conflicting views, the German government remains committed to the principle of short-time subsidies.

French employers are responsible for paying about half the wages lost by their employees during temporary reductions of working hours; they can then claim an 80 percent rebate of this amount from the government. As for Japan, reference has already been made to government subsidies of private payrolls to avoid layoffs of permanent employees.

If it could be shown that short-time employment subsidies are a cheaper means of handling temporary slack than standard unemployment compensation, that would constitute a powerful argument for it. But the open-ended nature of the system makes possible its abuse, whether intentional or inadvertent. How are employers to determine whether an economic slowdown is short or long term? If they apply for subsidies and there is still no work for all affected employees when the subsidy period comes to a close, the result will be that the duration of unemployment compensation has been extended and that the employees have lost time looking for other jobs. It is also possible that the employer might have been able to adjust operating schedules with few or no layoffs, had the crutch of part-time government subsidies not been available. Judging by their long experience and apparent satisfaction with the subsidy system, the German authorities seem to have been able to police it adequately.

FLEXIBLE HOURS

Flexible work hours, sometimes called flextime, involve a departure from the standard nine-to-five, five-day week. This may mean starting and quitting at different hours of the working day, with employees given some choice within limits set by management. Compressed work weeks (four ten-hour days, for example) are another variant. There are many other possibilities.

The flextime concept originated at a German aerospace company as a means of helping to solve rush hour traffic problems for employees. It is used most widely in Germany, where as many as 40 to 45 percent of all employees enjoy it. Growth has been more modest elsewhere. Flexible schedules were available to only 11.9 percent of the labor force in the United States in 1989, for 12.9 percent of the men and 10.6 percent of the women.[20] A growing number of Japanese firms are reported to be in the process of adopting it, including such giants as Mitsubishi Electric, Hitachi, and Toshiba.

The most common type of flextime is an arrangement that permits employees to set their own times for starting and quitting work, provided that they put in a full day (usually eight hours) and are at work at specified core hours during which all employees must be present. As a rule, once the choice is made, the schedule becomes fixed until amended by further negotiation.

Flextime is best suited to large service enterprises and to white-collar employees. In the United States, for example, it is most prevalent in trade, insurance, and real estate, and in the federal government. It is more difficult to arrange it for jobs such as line assembly in manufacturing establishments. In the United States, only 8.3 percent of manufacturing workers enjoyed the option of flextime in 1989.

The overwhelming majority of employees who have access to flextime like it. The advantages are obvious: they can avoid the worst commuting times; they can adjust their hours of work to family requirements; and they can do their shopping when stores are less crowded. It is particularly popular among married people with children. Professional and technical personnel are well represented among those who practice it.

The major advantage to employers is a more contented labor force, but there are problems that may account for its slow spread. Facilities may have to be kept open for longer periods with consequently higher utility and other overhead costs. There may have to be stricter time-keeping methods, and supervision may be more complicated. And there is the very critical consideration of ensuring that overall productivity does not suffer. For example, if there are two receptionists, you cannot allow both of them to take early schedules, leaving the desk empty in the late afternoon.

Data on costs are lacking, but presumably flextime would not be adopted if it were not cost effective, at least in the private sector. Germany may be an exception, in that its powerful works councils have actively promoted flextime; management may have been prepared to accommodate them at some cost, possibly in return for other concessions.

COMPRESSED WORK WEEKS

This is a form of flextime in which an employee completes a standard number of weekly working hours in less than five days. Typically it means that forty hours are compressed into four ten-hour days. Other possibilities include a four-and-a-half or even a three-day week. It is found mainly in entertainment and recreational services, in auto repair shops, and in health care and government.

The United States pioneered this scheme in the 1970s. Although its incidence has been rising, it is still fairly uncommon there, and even less usual in Europe. Its principal appeal is that it gives employees a longer weekend break. It reduces weekly commuting time and permits employees to engage in other activities, such as daytime attendance at educational institutions. Against this is the greater difficulty of family care on long working days and the element of fatigue. It is not feasible where heavy physical labor is required.

Employers have generally taken the initiative in introducing a compressed week. It can be an economically profitable system when the nature of product demand is favorable, because equipment and facilities may be more fully utilized. It is particularly cost effective if exemption from legal and contract overtime penalty rates can be secured.

There has also been a fairly high rate of abandonment of compressed weeks, attesting to its adoption under unfavorable circumstances. One development, however, may favor its wider use in the future. Not so many years ago, when the forty-eight hour week was standard, the six-day week was the norm. The five-day week was made possible by reduction of the working week to forty hours. When a standard thirty-six-hour week is reached, an event that may not be as far off as is often believed, a nine-hour, four-day week may become an attractive alternative to a seven-hour day. The introduction of the two-day weekend was a tremendous social event. While the marginal value of still another free day may be declining, there are undoubtedly many people who would be prepared to put in an extra hour a day to get it.

HOMEWORK

Homework differs from other forms of rearranged working time in that it is a practice of long standing and very controversial. The stereotype is that of a woman sewing garments in a dingy attic or cellar, earning very low wages, isolated from contact with other workers, and without the bargaining power afforded by trade union membership. It was largely under union pressure that the U.S. Department of Labor in the 1940s barred homework in a number of industries, including women's apparel, jewelry, gloves, and handkerchiefs.

A recent British survey indicated that nearly 1.7 million people, over 7 percent of the labor force, work at home in that country. Those engaged in manufacturing produced mainly clothing and similar products. Self-employed professionals and clerical workers were also well represented.

In 1985, the BLS made its first attempt to secure accurate data on the extent of homework in the United States, under the impetus of growing interest in this type of operation. A survey revealed that 8.4 million people were working at home for more than eight hours a week in non-farm occupations, thus constituting about 7.5 percent of the labor force. Of these, almost 1 million put in a thirty-five-hour week or more.[21]

It is interesting that there were more men than women homeworkers, although women averaged more hours a week than did the men. When it came to full-time workers, there were twice as many women as men. Services constituted by far the largest industry group, including educational, professional, business, repair, and social work. Altogether, 60 percent of the women and 35 percent of the men homeworkers were in one of these occupations. Trade and manufacturing were the next largest in terms of employment. Older people were represented disproportionately to their labor force participation.

Controversy has developed over a recent decision of the U.S. Department of Labor to eliminate the prohibitions on homework in five industries, including gloves, handkerchiefs, and jewelry. Employers who want to hire homeworkers in these industries will have to register with the department in order to make it possible to police minimum wage and child labor laws. Union officials called this step a "green light to exploit workers."[22] It is estimated by the BLS that at a maximum, 125,000 persons were engaged in the restricted industries, of whom only 20,000 worked thirty-five hours or more per week. In any event, it is hard to see that the newly freed industries have much of a future, given the lower labor costs in the less developed countries.

What has aroused most current interest in homework is the development of new computer and telecommunications technology, which makes it possible to tie home-based computers into central facilities at relatively low cost. The detailed record-keeping performed in banks, insurance companies, and brokerage firms, among others, can be farmed out to individuals working at home instead of their being assembled in large offices.

The proponents of the new technology point to a number of advantages for both employer and employee. Firms engaged in this type of operation have reported a 15 to 30 percent increase in productivity. Women whose family responsibilities require them to stay home can benefit from paid employment, and this would also be true of people with physical handicaps. The cost of office space is reduced. Greater flexibility to meet peak operating demands is also possible.

There are, however, difficulties that have led to what is believed to be a relatively small number of people doing this kind of work, although precise data are lacking. Equipment must be installed and maintained in homes, which may be more costly than in a central facility. If home operators are hired as independent contractors rather than employees, which is typically the case in the United States, they may not be covered by unemployment compensation or health insurance, and must bear the full cost of social security taxes. Since they are often paid by the piece, their income may be irregular, depending on the scheduling of the employer. Opportunities for career advancement are limited.

In general, homework will undoubtedly continue in those occupations where it is already well established—professional, technical, and repair services staffed by individual entrepreneurs. Many of these people work full- or part-time in regular establishments and do extra work on their own, sometimes to frustrate the income tax collector in countries with high marginal rates of taxation. Still, the future of home-based manufacturing is doubtful because the labor-intensive products that are usually produced have to compete with imports from less developed countries.

The future of teleworking is the most difficult to forecast. In view of the widespread ownership of small computers and the diffusion of knowledge about their use, it is somewhat surprising that homework of this kind has not grown more rapidly. Better child care facilities could slow its introduction, since many people prefer to work as part of a group rather than in isolation. Increased fertility rates would have the opposite effect. What telework does under appropriate circumstances is to afford the operator great flexibility in choosing hours of work. In this sense, it is a liberating force. There is no simple answer to the question of whether it will lead to the exploitation of labor, as the unions maintain. Homeworkers can protect themselves by refusing to work for substandard compensation, but they may have no alternative in depressed areas where there are few other regular employment opportunities.

SUMMARY

The many changes in working time practices that have taken place since World War II are due in large measure to the rapid growth of female labor force participation. In the United States, this rate rose from 38 percent in 1960 to 58 percent in 1989. Sweden has attained an even higher level than the United States, with Japan and Britain close behind. France and Germany are lagging, but they are inexorably moving in the same direction.

This sudden development ranks as one of the most important economic events of the twentieth century. With it came the realization that traditional patterns of work had to be modified to fit the needs of the new entrants into the labor market. Part-time work, job sharing, and flexible working hours are some of the responses that have occurred in the interest of a more productive use of labor resources.

As even more women seek paid employment—their participation rate in the United States is projected at 61.5 percent in the year 2000—the process of accommodation will have to continue. Sweden already permits paid post-maternity leave to be divided between mother and father, and similar arrangements may be possible for employment. For example, job sharing is an obvious arrangement when a married couple are in the same occupation, but only if employers are prepared to countenance it.

For men as well as women, one of the great unknowns is what will happen to the propensity to work as longevity increases. The United States has led the way in encouraging older people to remain in the labor market by banning compulsory retirement for age. Nonetheless, the participation rate for men aged sixty-five and over is projected to fall from 16 percent in 1987 to 10 percent by the year 2000. There is a tug of war between the desire for more leisure with growing affluence on the one hand and the psychological and economic pulls that make long years of full retirement unattractive for some people on the other. It would not be surprising if part-time work becomes a popular option for both sexes.

NOTES

1. See particularly John Owen, *Working Hours* (Lexington, Mass.: Lexington Books, 1979), and John Owen, *Reduced Working Hours: Cure for Unemployment or Economic Burden* (Baltimore: Johns Hopkins University Press, 1989). Robert A. Hart has also written extensively on the subject; a major study prepared for the OECD is cited below.

2. *Japan Labor Bulletin* (December 1988), p. 4.

3. Thomas J. Nardone, "Part-time Workers," *Monthly Labor Review* (February 1986), p. 16; Paul Blyton, *Changes in Working Time* (New York: St. Martin's Press, 1985), p. 103.

4. Unpublished data of the U.S. Bureau of Labor Statistics.

5. Bureau of National Affairs, *The Changing Workplace* (Washington: Bureau of National Affairs, 1986), p. 44.

6. European Trade Union Institute, *Flexibility of Working Time in Western Europe* (Brussels: European Trade Union Institute, 1986).

7. *Japan Labor Bulletin* (February 1989), pp. 5–8.

8. R. A. Hart, *Shorter Working Time* (Paris: OECD, 1984), p. 78.

9. Bureau of National Affairs, *Changing Workplace*, p. 63.

10. Ralf Dahrendorf and Eberhard Kohler, eds., *New Forms of Work and Activity* (Dublin: European Foundation for the Improvement of Work and Activity, 1986), p. 45; Alastair Evans and Tony Attew, "Alternatives to Full-Time Permanent Staff." In Chris Curson, ed., *Flexible Patterns of Work* (London: Institute of Personnel Management, 1986), pp. 110–112.

11. Simcha Ronen, *Alternative Work Schedules*, Homewood, IL: Dow-Jones Irwin, 1984), p. 182.

12. Joyce Epstein, "Issues in Job Sharing." In Dahrendorf and Kohler, *New Forms*, p. 79.

13. Japan Institute of Labor, *Japanese Working Life Profile* (Tokyo: Japanese Institute of Labor, 1988), p. 79.

14. Swedish National Social Insurance Board, *Social Insurance Statistics* (Stockholm: Swedish National Insurance Board, 1987), p. 60.

15. This section is based largely on an excellent survey paper: Bernard Casey, *Early Retirement Schemes With a Replacement Condition* (Berlin: International Institute of Management, 1985).

16. Ibid., pp. 15–18; Barry Alan Mirkin, "Early Retirement as a Labor Force Policy," *Monthly Labor Review* (March 1987), p. 30.

17. Japanese Institute of Labor, *Highlights in Japanese Industrial Relations*, Vol. 2 (Tokyo: The Japanese Institute of Labor, 1988), p. 29.

18. Mirkin, "Early Retirement," p. 32.

19. Jeremy Moon and J. J. Richardson, *Unemployment in the U.K.* (Aldershot: Gower Publishing, 1985), pp. 69–70.

20. Unpublished data of the U.S. Bureau of Labor Statistics.

21. Francis W. Horvath, "Work at Home," *Monthly Labor Review* (November 1986), p. 31.

22. *The New York Times*, November 11, 1988, p. 1.

Chapter Seven

THE SOVIET MODEL

Many of the labor market problems faced by the Soviet Union resemble those of the Western democracies, but its institutions and practices are quite different. The differences stem from the political and economic characters of the two systems as well as from their ideologies. To cite a fundamental contrast: Collective bargaining, as it is practiced in most Western countries, is premised on adversarial relationships between labor and capital, while the theory of Soviet labor relations posits a unity of interests between the two.

Until 1989, the Soviet model had wide application, but the political revolution that has occurred in the countries of Eastern Europe has led to a widespread restructuring of their labor markets and may move them nearer the West as central planning is replaced by markets. There has also been some change in the Soviet Union itself under the influence of *perestroika*. It is not yet clear what the final product will be like. The previous system had evolved over a period of seventy years, so alterations are likely to be incremental rather than sweeping. The following pages will describe the labor market arrangements that seemed so firmly established just a few years ago, as well as the challenges that have already led to some modifications.

There is still a single federation of labor in the Soviet Union, the All Union Central Council of Trade Unions (AUCCTU), consisting of thirty-two national unions organized along strict industrial lines. These in turn have regional and local branches blanketing the country. About 98 percent of all employees were union members at the last count, putting even the high union density of Sweden to shame.

What accounted for this extraordinary degree of organization in view of the fact that membership is not compulsory? The answer lies in the variety of trade union functions. In addition to representational activities, Soviet trade unions administer a wide range of economic, social, and cultural programs that are available only to members. In return for dues equal to 1 percent of their salaries, union members have access to union-sponsored housing and medical, vacation, and other benefits. The unions could well be described as quasi-governmental bodies that do much of the work allocated to labor and social security ministries in the West.

Almost all Soviet enterprises are still owned by the state, although cooperatives and joint ventures with foreign enterprises are beginning to make inroads. They are controlled by government ministries that are also organized along industrial lines. One of the goals of *perestroika* is to give individual enterprises full economic responsibility for the results of their activities. Some progress has been made in requiring financing through the enterprises' own resources, but there is still a long way to go in installing a market-based supply and demand system with uncontrolled prices.

Overall direction of labor market activities has been the responsibility of a government body, the State Committee for Labor and Social Problems. The general level and basic structure of wages have been determined by the central planning authorities and the industrial ministries, with the AUCCTU playing a consultative role. Wages and other conditions have been administered at the local level by enterprise trade union committees and management. The Gorbachev reforms aimed at a complete overhaul of the wage and salary structure, with increases to be determined by the ability of the individual enterprise to finance them, presumably on the basis of productivity. Things have not worked out as planned; in 1988, for example, wages rose by 7 percent on average while productivity went up only 5 percent, leading to a decision to have the banking system monitor wages to keep them in line.

In the pre–Gorbachev era, every Soviet institution—political, economic, and social—was under the direct control of the Communist Party. This included the trade unions at all levels, as well as management. Gorbachev appears to be determined to reduce the supervisory role of the Party, an initiative that is reportedly meeting strong opposition from the large Party bureaucracy, reluctant to see its powers and privileges diminished. What will eventually emerge is not clear; it will probably be some time before the dust has settled and the future of the Party determined.

INDUSTRIAL DEMOCRACY

It is a fixed principle of Soviet doctrine that workers are ensured of democracy at their places of work by the fact that all means of production are owned by the state, thus eliminating exploitation by private capitalists. The trade unions are regarded as adequate mechanisms to protect the parochial interests of employees against any possible infringement of their legal rights by management.

Not much is known about the precise role of the AUCCTU at the national level. Its chairpersons have usually been men with no previous union experience. They were always Communist Party functionaries, and on one occasion the head of the KGB was installed as chairman. The more recent tendency has been to promote career union officials to the post. There is some evidence that the AUCCTU does have influence over wage decisions, among other things, but as one study noted, "anecdotal evidence is not sufficient to prove that the unions actually influence labor policy. Perhaps all that can be said is that the AUCCTU and its departments and staff are one of several important political institutions involved in the formulation of Soviet labor policy."[1]

More is known about how unions operate at the local level. Their two main functions, which sometimes come into conflict, are to help raise productivity and to ensure that the legal and economic rights of employees are protected. The chief instrumentality of local activity is the factory committee, whose composition depends upon the size of the enterprise. Members are elected for one-year terms by the employees. In the past, candidates were usually selected by higher union echelons, and there was often only one candidate for each vacancy. This practice was increasingly condemned, even before the Gorbachev reforms, and elections have become more democratic.

The chairman of the factory committee is supposed to have equal authority with the plant manager in labor-related matters, and the committee itself participates in a wide range of administrative tasks through subcommittees. It appears, however, that the factory committee has played a subordinate role and that in the event of sharp conflict, the management view has prevailed.[2] The heightened militancy of workers may be forcing management to be more cautious in highly controversial matters.

The mutual obligations of labor and management are set down in collective agreements. These agreements are quite different from those prevalent in Western nations. They establish neither the level nor structure of wages, but are concerned mainly with such matters as plant safety, factory-financed housing, and cultural activities. The agreements commit the workforce to specified levels of output and to abiding by contractual work norms. They do not appear to be important in guaranteeing employee rights. Violations are frequent, particularly when management is under pressure to meet set production quotas. As one observer has noted, "data and testimonies reveal a tendency by both workers and management to set little store by the company contract. And when the new contract is presented to the workers' assembly, it is almost always approved *en masse*."[3]

Processing grievances is the local union's most important protective function and the one most closely related to industrial democracy. If individuals or groups complain of a violation of their legal or contract rights, the grievance is first heard by a joint labor-management shop commission and, if not resolved at that level, by a plant-wide Commission on Labor Disputes (KTS), which is also bipartite. If there is still no agreement, the matter goes to the full factory committee. Should the employee remain dissatisfied with the decision or if management does not concur, further appeal is possible. On questions of law, final resolution is made by the regular courts; on other issues, it is done by the regional trade union committees.

The procedure is well defined, but the question of how well it works remains. On the one hand, there is the view that consistent union failure to assist in redressing grievances would undermine their credibility and render them useless as instruments of labor discipline. It may also be true that maintaining employee morale and ensuring higher labor productivity demand that workers be afforded a meaningful avenue for airing complaints and obtaining relief. On the other hand, Soviet trade unions have been quasi-governmental bodies devoted primarily to the maintenance of discipline and high work norms. A resolution of these conflicting views has been reached as follows:

No one can deny the very limited nature of union democracy in the Soviet Union. On balance, central trade union and party officials have the ability to exert more pressure upon an enterprise union officer than do the workers with whom the officer must deal. . . . Does it mean that union officials will never take an action of benefit to workers? It does not. What it does mean is that union officials will be most likely to act on the workers' behalf when they perceive that their own interests and those of the Party coincide with that of the workers.[4]

The series of events that followed strikes by coal miners in Kuznetsk and the Don Basin in 1989 marked a new era in Soviet labor relations. The implications have still not played themselves out. The strike was long condemned as an inappropriate method of worker protest and illogical in a communist society. In striking against a state-owned enterprise, the workers were seen as in effect striking against themselves, since the state presumably represented their interests. Prior to the Gorbachev regime, sporadic work stoppages had been suppressed by police action. Under Gorbachev, occasional stoppages were settled by government mediation. For example, a sitdown strike at the large Yaroslavl Motor Works in December 1987, to protest the imposition of compulsory overtime work for twenty Saturdays a year, was settled by reducing the number of Saturdays to eight; in addition, the company management was fined for acting unilaterally.

The coal strike transcended anything that had taken place in the Soviet Union since the early years of Communist control. The entire labor force of the two largest coal-producing areas in the Soviet Union refused to work until their living conditions were improved. In order to get production started again, the government was forced to commit itself to a package of wage increases and consumer goods shipments that cost almost $5 billion out of an already strained budget.

To make matters worse, the miners acted through ad hoc strike committees rather than through their official local unions. They attempted to pressure the central committee of their national union into withdrawing from the AUCCTU and forming an independent organization, but were unable to achieve this goal. The entire episode was a clear demonstration of the miners' lack of confidence in the willingness and ability of the formal trade union set-up to improve their working conditions.

The government administrators reacted by proposing legislation to give them emergency authority to ban all strikes for a period of fifteen months. The legislature refused to go that far; instead it enacted legislation that established the legal right to strike but restricted the circumstances under which a strike could be called. All work stoppages were forbidden in public transportation, communications, and the power and defense industries, as well as where stoppages might threaten life or health. Also barred were strikes where continuous operations were essential to prevent damage to machinery and equipment, such as in steel mills. In other industries, preliminary to striking, workers were required to submit their grievances to an impartial mediatory body. If there were no agreement in five days, the parties could appeal for arbitration, and if the matter were not decided to their satisfaction in seven days, a strike could be called. Violation of these procedures would subject strikers to "disciplinary proceedings."

One thing is clear: Unless there is a counterrevolution and Grobachev is deposed, Soviet workers will no longer tolerate the level of industrial democracy afforded by the existing system. There are a number of alternative outcomes. The present government-controlled unions may seek the allegiance of workers by becoming more militant. That has already happened in Poland, where the old unions are outbidding Solidarity in their demands for higher wages. There is some evidence that this is occurring in the Soviet Union as well. In western Siberia, the major oil-producing region, the official trade unions have threatened to strike unless the government builds houses and guarantees wages for all workers, even those who may no longer be needed.

Another scenario is the establishment of a new labor federation in opposition to the AUCCTU. Leaders of the ad hoc committees of the coal miners have walked out of a congress of the national miners' union and are threatening to form an independent union. A third alternative is for the labor brigades (see below) to take over the economic functions of the unions and leave them with only social activities.

There have been attempts in the past to give workers the feeling that they had some voice in the operation of their enterprises. A 1973 statute required all enterprises with more than 300 employees to organize conferences that met quarterly and carried on interim tasks through elected executive committees. The latter were to have broad responsibilities to review production problems and suggest changes in the interest of efficiency. They suffered from vague agendas and insufficient opportunity for discussion. By all accounts, they have not given participants the impression that they had an active role in making managerial decisions.

A device intended to stimulate individual initiative as well as to augment employee participation is the system of work brigades, which have become the primary working units in manufacturing and construction. The brigades may be divided into working crews and are headed by an elected group leader. They often work on single assignments of a fairly long duration and are paid by results. Individual members are compensated according to their skills. Bonuses may be earned if the work is finished before the scheduled date.

There are claims that the brigade system has led to higher productivity, but supporting data are lacking. The brigades may have reduced manpower requirements and encouraged workers to upgrade their skills in order to take over for absent brigade members better. Brigades may elect a council to represent them in dealing with management, and they can arrange for the internal allocation of compensation. But the formation of the brigades and the assignment of work are subject to managerial control, so that they do not appear to have advanced the cause of industrial democracy.[5]

EMPLOYMENT AND UNEMPLOYMENT

Gainful employment in the West is a privilege available to all citizens, who must find work on their own to support themselves. If they are wealthy, they have the choice between work and leisure. The Soviet constitution gives everyone the right to a job, but there is also a corresponding legal obligation to work. Anyone capable of work who refuses to do so is subject to conviction for parisitism, a penal offense. Every so often there is an effort to catch people who have slipped through the net and may be engaged in dubious occupations, or none at all. In 1986, for example, every Moscow resident of working age was required to register with the city authorities. Those without legitimate excuses who were not working full-time or enrolled as students were offered assistance in securing employment. The names of those who refused to accept reasonable jobs were turned over to the police.

It is thus not surprising that labor force participation rates are high. This is particularly true of women, of whom about 80 percent have been gainfully employed in recent years. Part of the reason lies in demographic history. Because of the heavy loss of life among males during the Stalinist purges and World War II, there were more women than men in the labor force until the mid-1970s.

It has long been part of Soviet dogma that unemployment could not exist in a planned economy. There was thus no need for unemployment compensation. Indeed, manpower authorities continue to express concern over labor shortages. The growth of the population of working age slowed down sharply in the 1980s and will probably not accelerate during the coming decade.

Why are there complaints of a lack of manpower in the Soviet Union when unemployment is high in much of Western Europe? Several factors may be cited in explanation.

1. Unemployment does exist, but the manner in which it is usually handled keeps it hidden. Enterprises have been required to retain redundant employees on their payrolls until new jobs were found for them. Some employment offices have been set up to reduce the reemployment burden on enterprises, but this has not yet become the customary manner of effecting transitions to new jobs.

2. It has been estimated that Soviet labor turnover rates averaged about 20 percent per year, not far from Western rates. Soviet workers average a gap of twenty-eight working days between jobs. This frictional unemployment does not appear in Soviet statistics. A recent study based on interviews with Soviet emigres came up with a lower bound figure of 1.2 percent unemployment for recent years, most of it short-term.[6]

3. Even if this figure were doubled or tripled, it still represents a low level of unemployment by Western standards. Apart from the way in which it has been handled administratively, the maintenance of a consistently high demand for labor has contributed to the result. One of the principal causes of this phenomenon has been the practice of assigning production quotas to Soviet enterprises and measuring managerial success by their fulfillment. There were some labor cost constraints, but managers found ways of circumventing them. Hoarding of labor was common, as insurance against the fluctation in labor demand occasioned by uncertain delivery of materials, excessive absenteeism and turnover, and increases in production quotas. Skilled workers in particular could have been difficult to replace if they had been let go. The goal of maximizing output rather than profits virtually guaranteed a persistent manpower shortage.

This system has substantial costs. Labor productivity was low, since even employees who were not putting forth much effort were rarely discharged. There were many reports of people working at performance levels far below their capabilities: "according to one Moscow enterprise director, 80 percent of the potential of the average blue collar worker is exploited, but no more than 20 percent of the potential of the average engineer."[7]

A major objective of *perestroika* is to move profits into first place as the objective function of Soviet enterprise. This would reduce pressure on the labor market and give rise to greater unemployment. To ease worker fears, decrees enacted in 1988 provided for two months of advance notice of layoffs, one month's severance pay, and a maximum of two months on salary while the employee is looking for a new job. Unemployment compensation, job training, and special subsidies for the long-term unemployed are among the measures being considered to alleviate hardship. If these plans are implemented, the Soviet labor market will begin to resemble those of the West.

Warning that attaining higher productivity targets might mean the loss of between 13 and 19 million jobs by the end of the century, a Soviet economist has summarized the future unemployment problem as follows:

> The need to look for a job—a necessity that many now working in manufacturing and services will certainly face—may also be new and unaccustomed for us. We are used to the exact opposite—work seeking the person. . . . Obviously, considerable reorientation will be required. We consider it natural and necessary that if, through objective causes, a job slot becomes unnecessary, the worker must immediately be given another job. . . . Now we shall have to get used to the idea that finding employment is, to a considerable extent, the worker's own responsibility and that the search may require a certain amount of time—a sufficient but not an unlimited amount.[8]

RETIREMENT

The normal retirement age in the Soviet Union is sixty years for men and fifty-five years for women. On the average, men collect pensions for sixteen years and women for twenty-four years. Pension amounts are based on past earnings and length of employment, but with a ceiling. Thus, the pensions of high wage earners do not fully reflect the difference in their earnings. Pensions have been falling in relation to earnings; at present, the average pension is less than 50 percent of the average wage. There are no private pensions to supplement the state pension, although individual savings have been substantial, partly because of the unavailability of sufficient consumer goods to match incomes. There have been discussions of the need to raise pensions, but there is reluctance to do so because of the endemic labor shortage.

In some sectors of the economy, employees can receive both pensions and earnings; in others, they can opt for length of service additions to their earnings. But efforts to induce older people to remain at work are not much in evidence. Few part-time jobs are available; the option is working full-time or not at all. Jobs available to pensioners tend to be less interesting than those that they had held prior to retirement. Nevertheless, more than 60 percent of all those receiving pensions in 1986 continued to work during the first retirement year. The government appears to be torn between the desire to reduce inequities by raising pensions and the fear that to do so would discourage post-retirement work.

Retirement policy in the Soviet Union differs considerably from that in most Western nations. The Soviets do not encourage early retirement as a means of reducing unemployment, although the low retirement age may contribute to that end. In the absence of infirmity, there is an obligation to continue working until the pensionable age is reached. Extension rather than contraction of years of work appears to be the most likely path for Soviet citizens during the next decade at least. Because of past declines in birth rates and an increase in mortality, it is likely that the country will have greater need of the services of its older people.

WORKING TIME

With women constituting so large a portion of the Soviet labor force, it would seem logical for the authorities to make special arrangements for their time of work. They have not done so. Most Soviet women work full-time on regular schedules.

The standard pattern of working time in the Soviet Union is a forty-hour, five-day week. Only 0.6 percent of all employees were working part-time in 1983, and there has probably been little change since. Overtime work is a common occurrence and adds to the length of the week. Workers cannot refuse to perform it unless specifically exempted. A recent publication by the U.S. Department of Labor puts the *actual* average work week for blue-collar workers at forty-eight hours, but no data are presented to substantiate this figure.[9]

So much has been written about the plight of Soviet women in their dual role of housewives and paid employees that the subject is legendary by now. Household help is unavailable, and husbands traditionally offer little assistance at home. Women do most of the shopping, which is very time consuming because of the backwardness of retail services. The shortage of consumer goods makes queuing the norm. One result is a good deal of absenteeism during the working day, for employees may slip away from their jobs to shop when the lines are shorter. The employed housewife must do the cooking; the option of eating out is precluded by the lack of restaurants, and processed foods are generally unavailable.[10]

Facing low fertility rates, the Soviet Union has adopted measures designed to stimulate population growth. The most important of these is partially paid maternity leave of one-and-a-half years. Mothers receive lump sum payments that increase for each child up to the third and decline thereafter. The question of why part-time work is not made available to facilitate child care comes to mind.

Only invalids have a legal right to part-time work. For the rest, the policy appears to reflect the unwillingness to accept the economic cost that would result. Putting one-quarter of the female labor force on half time—a relatively low proportion by current Western standards—implies a loss of labor equivalent to 10 million full-time workers out of a labor force of 150 million. Managers are reluctant to sanction part-time work because of the tightness of the labor market and the fear that lifting the lid a bit might result in a flood of applicants for reduced hours.

Are these fears justified? Would a large number of women opt for part-time work if it were available? The major obstacle is economic. On the average, women earn about two-thirds as much as men. Nevertheless, their contribution to the household budget is critical, since Soviet wage levels are geared to the two-earner family. This was the mechanism by which Soviet women were induced to enter the labor force in the first place.

Surveys have suggested that 90 percent of those who would like to work part-time are women, but only about 10 percent of them are prepared to suffer the loss of income.[11] There is no way of determining in advance what would actually happen, and the Soviet authorities do not appear disposed to experiment. If the Gorbachev reforms succeed in reducing labor demand and if the level of real incomes rises in accordance with the plans, the availability of part-time work might become feasible.

There has been some recent government encouragement of homework where it is difficult for women to reach factories and offices. What little is known of homeworkers suggests that there are few of them and that they are engaged mainly in the manufacture of garments. Legislation has been enacted to facilitate the process. Telework awaits the future, since personal computers are few and far between in the Soviet Union.

The status of women retirees raises some interesting questions. They are eligible for pensions at age fifty-five and have a longer life expectancy than men, yet a smaller proportion of women than men retirees are in the labor force. One reason seems to be what may be termed the grandmother effect. So heavy is the burden on working women that older women are pressed into service to care for children and help with the housework. The shortage of housing makes this easier, since it is not unusual for grown children and parents to have to live together. For the Soviet Union as a whole, the average amount of living space per capita is about 110 square feet, which means that a family of five (working parents, two children, and a grandmother) would have 550 square feet of living space—close quarters. Having a built in babysitter may compensate for the inconvenience.

SOCIALIST COMPETITION

At least brief mention should be made of a unique practice that is a heritage from Stalinist days. As originally conceived, this involved challenges from one group of workers to another, or from one factory to another, to raise output, with suitable rewards to the victors in the form of medals, bonuses, and trips to Moscow. The peak of the movement was reached when a coal miner named A. G. Stakhanov over-fulfilled his shift quota by 1400 percent. He thus gave rise to the Stakhanovite movement in which individual workers were urged to emulate the so-called Heroes of Labor in the achievement of prodigious feats of output. This involved a speedup of working tempo and eventually lost its effectiveness.

It has survived in a less frenetic form, however. Individuals are now urged to take an active role in helping to raise production. This includes making personal pledges that fixed quotas will be met. The members of a labor brigade or the entire personnel of a factory may agree to achieve specified production targets and share in any excess profits to the enterprise resulting from the effort.

As far as can be judged, this practice does not appear to have had any significant incentive effects or impact on productivity. Several studies have found that a fair number of workers are active participants in this form of socialist competition—a figure of 38 percent of the labor force was cited for an automobile factory—but whether this has translated into higher output was not indicated. The Soviet "rate buster" is probably no more popular with his peers than his counterpart in the West. The difference is that Soviet trade unions encourage this activity, whereas it would be suicidal for a Western trade union to do so.

The Soviet Union has little to teach the West so far as labor market practices are concerned. The Soviet conception of industrial democracy would have few adherents among Western workers. Some might regard the elimination of long-term unemployment in the Soviet Union as a major achievement, but the cost is high in terms of economic efficiency. It is paradoxical that the self-proclaimed workers' state should do so little to reduce the burdens on its working women. Gorbachev has committed the country to doubling the output of goods and services by the end of the century. This might be easier to achieve if the Soviet labor market were reorganized along Western lines.

NOTES

1. Blair A. Ruble, *Soviet Trade Unions* (Cambridge, U.K.: Cambridge University Press, 1981), p. 41.

2. Bruno Grancelli, *Soviet Management and Labor Relations* (London: Allen & Unwin, 1988), p. 131.

3. Ibid., p. 131.

4. Blair A. Ruble, "Factory Unions and Workers' Rights." In Arcadius Kahan and Blair A. Ruble, eds., *Trade Unions in Communist States* (Elmsford, NY: Pergamon Press, 1979), p. 73.

5. For a discussion of the brigade system, see Meredith M. Heinemeier, "The Brigade System of Labor Organization and Incentives in Soviet Industry and Construction." In U.S. Congress, 100th Congress, 1st Session, Joint Economic Committee, *Gorbachev's Economic Plans*, Vol. 2, November 23, 1987 (Washington: GPO), pp. 272–281.

6. Paul R. Gregory and Irwin L. Collier, Jr., "Unemployment in the Soviet Union," *American Economic Review* (September 1988), p. 613.

7. U.S. Congress, 100th Congress, 1st Session, Joint Economic Committee, November 23, 1987 (Washington: GPO), p. 225.

8. Ibid., p. 235.

9. U.S. Department of Labor, "The Union of Soviet Socialist Republics," *Foreign Labor Trends* (1989), p. 3.

10. For a good survey of the economics of the Soviet household, see William Moskoff, *Labor and Leisure in the Soviet Union* (New York: St. Martin's Press, 1984).

11. Ibid., pp. 30–31.

Chapter Eight

SUMMARY AND CONCLUSIONS

The list of labor market institutions covered in this volume is far from comprehensive. Such major subjects as wage structure and collective bargaining were not included because their importance has resulted in a voluminous literature that could not have been summarized in a study of modest proportions. Less is known about the programs and practices described in this volume, despite their impact on the well-being of the people whom they affect.

It was also not possible to include all the countries whose experience is interesting and valuable, among them Italy, the Netherlands, Canada, Australia, Denmark, and Norway. The rationale for the set of countries selected is that they typify diverse approaches to a set of common problems and have been innovators in important areas. In addition, they are also major economic powers. The inclusion of the Soviet Union for comparative purposes hardly requires justification.

It is difficult to determine with any degree of precision how any particular labor practice affects the country. Partial evaluations, mainly in the form of cost/benefit analyses, have been cited when they were available, which was not too frequently because of problems of quantifying them. For example, how does one measure the loss suffered by a worker who is suddenly discharged from a position that he or she has held for many years and expected to occupy until retirement? Deprivation of income is only part of it. Psychological disorientation may be more damaging, yet it is difficult to place a value on anything but income. To cite another example, how are the benefits of improved employee morale, which result from a better quality of working life or participation in managerial decisions, to be measured? Productivity is not a sufficient criterion, since it is dependent on many other factors that are hard to hold constant. Quality of output, care exercised in using cooperating capital equipment, or a heightened sense of responsibility for the success of the enterprise resulting in more innovation—these are among the variables that should be put into the equation.

Occasionally there is a factor of sufficient importance in itself to manifest an independent effect. The poor performance of the British economy during several postwar decades was often attributed, at least in part, to the lack of an adequate means of averting frequent though short stoppages of work. The result was that orderly production scheduling was almost impossible. One of the first actions of the Conservative government led by Margaret Thatcher was to enact remedial legislation to curb this most inefficient manner of settling grievances. Other practices that were dealt with in the previous chapters do not lend themselves to so clear an interpretation.

Among these fairly novel practices, codetermination stands out. As practiced in Germany and to a modified extent in the Scandinavian countries and the Netherlands, it represents a compromise between traditional capitalist enterprise, in which management has an untrammeled right to make business decisions unilaterally, and the producer cooperatives of the past, in which all decisional authority was vested in the employees. A variant of the latter is the postwar Yugoslav system of workers' ownership, which has not proved to be an economic success.

At the corporate level, codetermination provides employee representatives with full information about company operations and plans. This helps to further a better understanding among the employees of the problems facing the enterprise. The exact number of employee representatives who sit on boards of directors under this scheme is not of critical importance; the current efforts of the German trade unions to gain full parity may be misplaced. The arrangement is not likely to work well if the parties cannot reach a consensus, no matter what the majority vote of the board. If management representatives are prepared to listen to the views of their employee colleagues, to give them careful consideration, and to accept compromises where feasible, formal votes may not even be necessary, except as a matter of record.

Plant-level works councils have played an equally important role under codetermination. They may be even more significant in that they bring information closer to the individual employee and provide him with a greater sense of participation in the affairs of the enterprise. Although German works councils do not have decisional authority except for certain personnel matters, the corporate executive who does not consult his works council on non-routine actions is borrowing trouble. On the other side, employees who perceive that their employment security is enhanced because no job-threatening action will be taken without their knowledge and without giving them an opportunity to present alternative solutions to projected layoffs are more likely to be loyal to the enterprise and more conscientious in performing their work. Their ideas may be of considerable value to the company; an impersonal suggestion box is no substitute for full discussion.

Employers in countries without any type of codetermination, the United States in particular, tend to argue that a dilution of managerial responsibility is not compatible with efficient corporate operation. They assert that decisions often must be made quickly and without any publicity. These conditions may be difficult to fulfill if preliminary discussion outside a small managerial group is required. Plans for mergers, opening or closing plants, new product lines, or price changes, among other things, might be compromised.

It can be said, however, that industry has performed well under codetermination in Germany and Sweden. There appears to be little disposition on the part of businessmen in either country to complain that codetermination has undermined their capacity to make decisions with reasonable speed or has frustrated their ability to make essential operating adjustments. The system, at least as practiced in these two countries, has not proved incompatible with the efficient operation of private enterprise. It has not led to deadlock or heightened industrial strife. Neither German nor Swedish employers would welcome complete parity between labor and owner representatives in the management of corporate affairs, but the present ratios of representation appear to be satisfactory. It should not be forgotten that in the event of irreconcilable disagreements, the management view does prevail.

Codetermination is not for every country under present conditions. It works best where there are powerful and responsible trade unions. If employers challenge the very legitimacy of trade unions and prefer to operate on a nonunion basis, as many do in the United States, the necessary cooperative relationships may be impossible to achieve. Moreover, such employers are not likely to concede board representation and works councils in the absence of unusual circumstances, such as an impending bankruptcy that can be staved off only with union cooperation. The strong class feelings that persist in countries like France and Britain are also obstacles to close relationships between labor and management.

Trade unions have been cautious about embracing the codetermination concept. Special circumstances in Germany created a favorable union attitude there, but elsewhere the view persists that union officials cannot simultaneously serve their members and their employers without compromising the interests of one or both. These officials are concerned that, by embracing some degree of managerial responsibility, they may alienate their constituents and be displaced by less responsible opponents. This is a real possibility where there are strong left-wing unions or factions within unions, as in France and Britain, but this is a problem of leadership. The rank and file must be convinced that their interests are best served by cooperation rather than conflict. This may not be easy to do.

Employee stock ownership is no substitute for codetermination. The gap between ownership and control is too great. Individual stockholders have little influence over policy in widely held public companies; under most ESOP arrangements, even the combined holdings of employees would not carry much weight. Nor is stock ownership likely to provide much of an incentive factor, since it is difficult for an individual employee to see the connection between his efforts and the value of his holdings. Stock bonuses to corporate executives are another matter, for the rewards are large and immediate if things go well.

The history of the ESOP concept is not encouraging. An earlier variant was popular in the United States during the 1920s, but disappeared when the stock market crashed in 1929. The market decline in 1987 may have had a similar chilling effect as employee stockholders saw their nest eggs shrinking. Contrary to the slogan of its boosters, ESOP is not likely to make every worker a capitalist.

The Swedish stock ownership funds suffer from similar drawbacks. To the individual employee, the stock fund is just another pension fund, remote from his everyday life and not likely to improve his incentive to work. The wider implication of the scheme—eventual control of large blocks of corporate stock by trade unions—opens vistas of a syndicalist society. The plan appears to have little future outside Sweden. Even there, the usually complacent employers continue to oppose it and intend to bring about its repeal if the Socialists lose governmental power.

The Quality of Working Life movement has two main objectives—job enrichment and higher productivity. Its appeal to employers and employees depends on where the emphasis is placed. Japan has pioneered in the establishment of quality circles, which are small groups of employees dedicated primarily to improving both the quality and quantity of output with job enrichment playing little if any role. By all accounts, this movement has accomplished its purpose in Japan. Labor productivity in manufacturing has risen rapidly. This effect has attracted American employers, primarily in the automobile industry, which faces stiff Japanese competition. The emphasis on productivity has led American trade unions to take a reserved attitude toward QWL, lest it be another name for an old-fashioned speed-up.

By contrast, the Swedish concept of QWL stresses job enrichment, although its potential for raising productivity has not been ignored. The Volvo experiment with work rearrangement has aroused considerable interest in Europe, but what hinders replication is the substantial capital investment required for its installation. The Volvo initiative was an act of faith, and, while it appears to have paid off, the rewards have not been great. What first aroused the interest of Volvo was the difficulty of recruiting sufficient labor to perform boring, repetitive, stressful work on the assembly line. The high levels of unemployment that have prevailed in Europe during the 1980s and the fact that automobile plants operating with traditional methods generally pay good wages have meant that there was little pressure on employers to venture into Swedish job enrichment.

Industrial restructuring brought in its wake the loss of seemingly secure, well-paid jobs and has heightened interest in employment tenure. Japanese lifetime commitment has been seen as a possible model for other countries, but this practice is far from a panacea. Even in Japan, it is confined to a minority of workers employed by large firms. Temporary employees, women, and the employees of subcontractors are ordinarily not included. The age of compulsory retirement is low, somewhere between fifty-five and sixty years, so that lifetime is hardly an accurate characterization.

In general, the only employees covered by the guarantee are those hired directly from school. They do not have the option of changing employers, for the guarantee does not follow them. They are required to accept intrafirm mobility at the behest of their company, even if moves to new locations disruptive to the family are involved. A young man who enters this sheltered employment milieu faces a lifetime career with a single enterprise. A fair number of them leave to find what they consider to be more congenial jobs in a less structured environment.

The system does inspire loyalty to the firm, since the employees are aware that their future is bound up with the firm's progress. One of the consequences is that the basic unit of trade union structure is the individual enterprise, so that national unions spanning more than one firm have little power. Frequently, the enterprise unions are headed by supervisory personnel who are not likely to challenge management. This has resulted in the almost complete absence of ordinary economic strikes. It has been thirty years since there has been a genuine work stoppage of substantial duration in Japan. Some may regard this as favorable result; it certainly says something about the Japanese labor movement.

Japanese management prides itself on its concern for the welfare of its employees and maintains that the wages and other prevailing labor conditions are the maximum that can be afforded. It should be noted, however, that the annual number of hours worked in Japan is considerably higher than in the United States or Western Europe. Moreover, what an enterprise can afford to pay its employees is an elastic concept. In the West, it is determined by bargaining conducted on the employee side by national trade unions staffed by professional officials whose concerns transcend those of a single enterprise.

The Japanese employment system is not for export. It implies a degree of employer paternalism that most working people in the West would be reluctant to accept. Japanese firms have been able to sustain it because of their high and consistent economic growth, as well as government payroll support in periods of recession. There is also a buffer provided by the pool of non-regular employees who can be laid off at the will of the firm. These employees are second-class citizens who are not even eligible to become members of the enterprise unions, a status that Western trade unions would be unlikely to tolerate.

Other countries have tried to protect employment tenure by making layoffs difficult or expensive. The National Redundancy Fund in Britain, which is supplemented by individual employer payments, provides fairly generous severance pay. This has led to a higher rate of non-controversial separations than might have been expected and has facilitated staff reduction in declining industries. In a sense, employees build up equities in jobs that can be cashed in if the necessity arises.

France installed a system that required the approval of a government agency before a mass layoff could take place, but this proved cumbersome and was discontinued. It was replaced by so-called job conversion allowances distinct from ordinary unemployment compensation. The allowance finances leave while the employee is waiting to be recalled or undergoing training for the acquisition of new skills. A considerable degree of job protection is afforded in Germany by the requirements that layoffs must be discussed with works councils before being put into effect and that a "social plan" designed to minimize hardship must be adopted. There is no statutory right to severance pay in the United States, although many union contracts require it. The only job protection available to most American employees is a sixty-day advance notice of mass layoffs or plant closures, and even that is hedged about with restrictions.

The Soviet Union requires all able-bodied citizens to work and provides *de facto* job tenure. This does not mean that a worker is guaranteed employment with a particular enterprise, but, at least in the past, redundant workers were retained by their firms until other jobs could be found for them. One of the results was slack work practices. The Soviet authorities are currently considering toleration of unemployment as a means of improving work effort.

Employment security is a high priority issue for those who stand to lose their jobs as a result of industrial restructuring. Permanent tenure does not appear to be an option in dynamic economies in which labor mobility is essential for the efficient allocation of the labor force. Recognizing that some unemployment, even if transitory, is unavoidable, most countries have initiated policies designed to soften its impact and to minimize the duration of the transition to new jobs. The most ambitious is Sweden, where an "active labor market" policy has aroused a great deal of international interest. All vacancies in that country are reported to local employment offices where they are computerized, so that a national inventory of available jobs is on hand when an unemployed worker appears to claim his or her benefits. If an appropriate vacancy cannot be found immediately, a selection of training courses is offered. If the individual is willing to move to another locality, the employment system is prepared to pay travel and moving expenses.

The core of the Swedish system is a dense network of employment offices sufficiently well staffed that every applicant can receive adequate attention. That is the main obstacle to its adoption elsewhere—it is very expensive. To the Swedes, full employment is a national priority, and they are willing to pay the cost. Few other nations are prepared to do so. The United States, for example, despite legislation on the books calling for full employment, does not have a national employment office system. Each separate state has its own employment service, which is usually poorly funded and able to do little more than process unemployment benefit checks. European countries tend to do better, but none has gone as far as Sweden.

Britain is second to Sweden in government efforts to minimize unemployment. It has a comprehensive network of job centers through which a number of schemes have been tried. These include community temporary job creation programs, subsidies to unemployed individuals and employers to encourage hiring, and skill training, among others. Nevertheless, the impact on unemployment has not been substantial. Britain suffers from a regional and occupational maldistribution of its labor force; there is a good deal of blue-collar unemployment in the northern part of the country, while at the same time there are white-collar vacancies in the south.

The United States and Germany have relied primarily on a combination of training and public sector jobs to reduce unemployment. The United States has generally used a pattern of block grants from the federal government to the states to finance local public job creation and training programs. There has not been a large commitment of funds for these purposes, nor do the programs appear to have been a significant factor in reducing unemployment. The German training schemes have been larger and more comprehensive, with high rates of completion and post-training placement. German programs have differed from those of the United States with respect to both the scale and availability of an effective employment service to administer them.

Reviewing the melange of government programs that have been instituted to deal with the often high levels of unemployment during the 1970s and 1980s, it must be said that no really satisfactory solution has been found. Keynesian macroeconomic intervention, which received enthusiastic support during the halcyon days of the 1960s, fell into disfavor in the subsequent period of stagflation (simultaneous inflation and unemployment). Governments have become wary of applying economic stimulants for fear of setting off price increases, which appear to be more seriously damaging politically than unemployment.

Rapid economic growth plus occasional employment subsidies can keep unemployment down, as the Japanese have shown, but this happy alternative is difficult to achieve.

Direct intervention in the labor market can eliminate unemployment, but the cost is prohibitive for countries that are not really dedicated to the maintenance of full employment; this is the lesson of the Swedish experience. But full employment may also carry in its wake pernicious effects on work incentives and on the optimum allocation of labor resources. What has thus far eluded economic policymakers is the happy medium: a desirable degree of labor mobility, combined with cost effective measures that provide productive and remunerative work for those whose job loss serves a socially useful function.

The failure thus far to find an answer to the unemployment paradox does not mean that direct labor market measures should be abandoned. They have provided temporary assistance to a great many people and helped others to find permanent employment. What is warranted is a comprehensive analysis of two decades of experience with a wide variety of programs, in order to determine whether an optimal mix of training and retraining, public job creation, subsidies to private firms, unemployment compensation, and other governmental initiatives can be found. The lessons of the last two decades cannot be construed to support the conclusion that the problem of unemployment is best handled by market forces alone.

The pattern of working time has emerged as a major issue largely because of the rapidly expanding proportion of women entering the labor market. Traditionally, the burden of domestic tasks fell upon women, and this has been slow to change. Women with small children find it difficult to care for them while holding full-time jobs. Day care centers help, but they are inadequate everywhere, even in the most advanced welfare states.

The response of the labor market has been part-time work. Fixed labor costs in the form of per capita social insurance taxes are the chief drawbacks for the employer, but these can be alleviated by apportioning the tax to hours worked rather than on a straight per capita basis. Part-time work has the advantage that employment can be adjusted more readily to meet peak demands; this is particularly true for retail establishments.

Another innovation has been job sharing. This is difficult to arrange, since it requires the cooperation of individuals with similar if not identical skills. It is particularly useful for highly skilled occupations in which labor is in short supply; nursing is a good current example. For sharing to be possible, there must be a vacancy for one full-time employee, and the employer must be willing to accept often complicated personnel adjustments.

An aspect of working time that is currently in a state of flux is the number of years that people remain in the work force before retiring. There are forces working in opposite directions: increasing affluence and improved pensions induce earlier retirement, while greater longevity encourages its postponement. Weighing in on the side of earlier retirement are reductions in force during recessions, accompanied by special governmental programs designed to make retirement more attractive in order to alleviate unemployment. This may take the form of subsidizing employers who agree to replace retired workers. Programs of this kind have been tried in Germany, Britain, and France, apparently without making much of a dent on unemployment.

Long-term demographic factors favor continuing labor force participation for older people. Declining rates of population growth imply the aging of the work force and consequently an increasing need for the services of the elderly, as well as the desirability of reducing the burden of pensions. The United States has gotten a headstart on other nations by banning entirely the imposition of compulsory retirement for reasons of age.

Flexible working hours are a response to the inconvenience of rush hour commuting and to the need to perform household tasks in families where there are two wage earners. Compressed work weeks are occasionally to be found but will probably be more common in the future, when weekly hours are further reduced, making nine-hour days and four-day work weeks attractive. The five-day week is of relatively recent origin—it is not yet universal in Japan—and there is no reason to doubt that rising economic productivity will be reflected in more leisure as well as higher income.

Paid work performed at home is controversial, for it recalls the exploitation of labor, particularly women, in the past. What may make this a rational and more widespread form of work in the future is the possibility of decentralizing routine clerical jobs through the use of home computers linked to a central facility. This has the potential of making work feasible for those unable to reach an office because of physical handicaps or the press of domestic responsibilities.

The general conclusions to be drawn from looking at some of the complex labor market institutions around the world depend largely on the preferences of the evaluator. No single set of practices stands out as so superior to all others as to merit unquestioning imitation. If that were so, there would be more international uniformity than now prevails.

If, however, industrial democracy is accepted as a critical component of modern industrial relations, the German system of codetermination merits serious consideration by other countries. It has worked well and represents an interesting compromise between socialism and free market capitalism. It is the most successful of the experiments designed to extend political democracy to the work place that have been tried during the past century.

If the reduction of unemployment is accorded a high priority, the Swedish labor market policy has a lot to offer. It preserves labor mobility without placing all the burden on those who must change jobs involuntarily in mid-career. It does not run counter to prevailing notions of appropriate governmental action but merely extends it. The principal drawback is cost, though the Swedes have found the policy to be economically efficient.

If a high value is placed on continuity of employment, both because of its hedonic aspects and its contribution to productivity, some version of the system of lifetime employment that exists in Japan might well be considered. The special circumstances that have facilitated the employment guarantee in Japan may not be present in other countries, but modified forms have actually been practiced by large enterprises elsewhere. It is also well to remember that substantial groups of employees already enjoy *de facto* or *de jure* job tenure in many countries, notably in government service.

For the rest, Quality of Working Life plans offer the promise of better working conditions. The proponents of this approach are quite active and its merits are well known. Adjustments of working hours are taking place without any special advocacy, largely in response to the rapid increase in the number of women who work for pay. Some interesting variations deserve closer attention than they have received, notably job sharing and the rearrangement of the work week, in the interest of less time spent in commuting, particularly in crowded urban areas.

BIBLIOGRAPHY

Berghan, Volker R., and Detlev Karsten. *Industrial Relations in West Germany*. Hamburg: Berg, 1987.

Blinder, Allen S. "Pay, Participation, and Productivity." *Brookings Review* (Winter 1989/90): pp. 33–38.

Blyton, Paul. *Changes in Working Time*. New York: St. Martin's Press, 1985.

Bosworth, Barry, and Alice M. Rivlin, eds. *The Swedish Economy*. Washington: Brookings Institution, 1987.

Bureau of National Affairs. *The Changing Workplace*. Washington: Bureau of National Affairs, 1986.

———. *Employee Stock Ownership Plans*. Washington: Bureau of National Affairs, 1987.

Casey, Bernard. *Early Retirement Schemes With a Replacement Condition*. Berlin: International Institute of Management, 1985.

Clegg, Hugh. *The Changing System of Industrial Relations in Great Britain*. Oxford: Basil Blackwell, 1979.

Cochran, Gus. *A Decade of Joint Regulation of Working Life in Sweden*. Stockholm: *Swedish Information Service* (Bulletin No. 34), 1987.

Commons, John R. et al. *History of Labor in the United States*. New York: Macmillan, Vol. II, 1946.

Cross, Michael, ed. *Managing Workforce Reduction*. New York: Praeger, 1985.

Curson, Chris, ed. *Flexible Patterns of Work*. London: Institute of Personnel Management, 1986.

Dahrendorf, Ralf, and Eberhard Kohler, eds. *New Forms of Work and Activity*. Dublin: European Foundation for the Improvement of Work and Activity, 1986.

Ellenberger, James N. "Japanese Management: Myth or Magic." *American Federationist* (April-June 1982): pp. 3–12.

Epstein, Joyce. "Issues in Job Sharing." Ed. Ralf Dahrendorf and Eberhard Kohler. *New Forms of Work and Activity*. Dublin: European Foundation for the Improvement of Work and Activity, 1986.

European Trade Union Institute. *Flexibility of Working Time in Western Europe*. Brussels: European Trade Union Institute, 1986.

Evans, Alastair, and Tony Attew. "Alternatives to Full-Time Permanent Staff." Ed. Chris Carson. *Flexible Patterns of Work*. London: Institute of Personnel Management, 1986.

Eyraud, François, and Robert Tchobanian. "The Auroux Reforms and Company Level Industrial Relations in France." *British Journal of Industrial Relations* (July 1985): pp. 241–259.

Farnham, David, and John Pimlott. *Understanding Industrial Relations*. London: Cassell, 1983.

Fuerstenberg, Friedrich. "Industrial Relations in the Federal Republic of Germany." Ed. Greg J. Bamber and Russell D. Lansbury. *International and Comparative Industrial Relations*. London: Allen & Unwin, 1987.

Gennard, John. "Great Britain," Ed. Edward Yemin. *Workforce Reductions in Undertakings*. Geneva: International Labor Office, 1982.

Goetschy, Janine, and Jacques Rogot, "French Industrial Relations." Ed. Greg J. Bamber and Russell D. Lansbury. *International and Comparative Industrial Relations*, London: Allen & Unwin, 1987.

Gordon, Allen. *Redundancy in the 1980s*. Aldershot: Gower Publishing, 1984.

Grancelli, Bruno. *Soviet Management and Labor Relations*. London: Allen & Unwin, 1988.

Gregory, Paul R. and Irwin L. Collier, "Unemployment in the Soviet Union." *American Economic Review* (September 1988): pp. 613–632.

Gyllenhammar, Per. *People at Work*. London: Addison-Wesley Publishing, 1977.

Hart, R. A. *Shorter Working Time*. Paris: Organization for Economic Cooperation and Development, 1984.

Heinemeier, Meredith M. "The Brigade System of Labor Organization and Incentives in Soviet Industry and Construction." In U.S. Congress, 100th Congress, 1st Session, Joint Economic Committee. *Gorbachev's Economic Plans*. Vol. 2. Washington: GPO, November 23, 1987.

Horvath, Francis W. "Work at Home." *Monthly Labor Review* (November 1986).

Inagami, Takeshi. *Labor-Management Communication at the Workshop Level*. Tokyo: The Japan Institute of Labor, 1983.

————. *Japanese Workplace Industrial Relations*. Tokyo: The Japan Institute of Labor, 1988.

Ishikawa, Kaoro. *Quality Control Circles at Work.* Tokyo: Asian Productivity Organization, 1984.

Jacobi, Otto. "World Economic Changes and Industrial Relations in the Federal Republic of Germany." In *Industrial Relations in a Decade of Industrial Change.* Madison, Wis: Industrial Relations Research Association, 1985.

Jallada, Jean-Pierre. *Toward a Policy of Part Time Employment.* Maastricht, The Netherlands: European Center of Work and Society, 1984.

Japanese Institute of Labor. *Highlights in Japanese Industrial Relations.* Vol. 2. Tokyo: Japanese Institute of Labor, 1988.

Japanese Institute of Labor. *Japanese Working Life Profile.* Tokyo: Japanese Institute of Labor, 1988.

Joyce, John T. "Expanding Economic Democracy." *An Issue Paper from Social Democrats USA,* 1988. Mimeograph.

Kahan, Arcadius, and Blair A. Ruble. *Trade Unions in Communist States.* Elmsford, N.Y.: Pergamon Press, 1979.

Katz, Harry C., Thomas A. Kochan and Kenneth Gobeille. "Industrial Relations Performance, Economic Performance, and QWL Programs." *Industrial and Labor Relations Review* (October 1983): pp. 3–33.

Kochan, Thomas A., Harry C. Katz, and Robert B. McKersie. *The Transformation of American Industrial Relations.* New York: Basic Books, 1986.

Kochan, Thomas A., Harry C. Katz, and Nancy R. Mower. *Worker Participation and American Unions.* Kalamazoo, Mich.: Upjohn Institute, 1984.

Koshiro, Kazutoshi. "The Quality of Working Life in Japanese Factories." In *Contemporary Industrial Relations in Japan.* Ed. Taishiro Shirai. Madison: University of Wisconsin Press, 1983.

Kuwahara, Yasuo. "The Process of Job Creation and Job Destruction in Japanese Industry." *Japan Labor Bulletin.* March 1988.

Lewis, Paul. *Twenty Years of Statutory Redundancy Payments in Great Britain.* Nottingham, U.K.: Universities of Leeds and Nottingham, 1985.

Maki, Omori. "Women Workers and the Japanese Industrial Relations System." Ed. Joachim Bergmann and Shigeyoshi Tokunaga. *Economic and Social Aspects of Industrial Relations.* Frankfurt: Campus Verlag, 1987.

Markovitz, Andrei S. *The Politics of West German Trade Unions.* Cambridge, U.K.: Cambridge University Press, 1986.

Meyerson, Per Martin. *The Welfare State in Crisis: The Case of Sweden.* Stockholm: Federation of Swedish Industries, 1982.

Mirkin, Barry Alan. "Early Retirement as a Labor Force Policy." *Monthly Labor Review* (March 1987): pp. 19–33.

Moon, Jeremy, and J. J. Richardson. *Unemployment in the U.K..* Aldershot: Gower Publishing, 1985.

Moskoff, William. *Labor and Leisure in the Soviet Union.* New York: St. Martin's Press, 1984.

Mouriaux, Marie Françoise, and René Mouriaux. "Unemployment Policy in France, 1976–82." Ed. Jeremy Richardson and Roger Henning. *Unemployment,* London: Sage Publications, 1984.

Nardone, Thomas J. "Part-Time Workers." *Monthly Labor Review* (February 1986): pp. 13–19.

National Commission for Employment Policy. *The Job Training Partnership Act.* Washington: GPO, 1987.

Nollen, Stanley D. *New Work Schedules in Practice.* New York: Van Nostrand Reinhold, 1982.

Organization for Economic Cooperation and Development. *Marginal Employment Subsidies.* Paris: OECD, 1982.

———. *A Challenge for Income Support Policies.* Paris: OECD, 1984.

———. *Economic Surveys: France.* Paris: OECD, 1986–87.

———. *OECD in Figures.* Paris: OECD, 1988.

Owen, John. *Working Hours.* Lexington, Mass.: Lexington Books, 1979.

———. *Reduced Working Hours.* Baltimore: Johns Hopkins University Press, 1989.

Rehn, Gosta. "Swedish Active Labor Market Policy," *Industrial Relations,* 24 (1985): pp. 62–89.

Ronen, Simcha. *Alternative Work Schedules.* Homewood, Ill.: Dow-Jones Irwin, 1984.

Ruble, Blair A. "Factory Unions and Workers' Rights." Ed. Arcadius Kahn and Blair A. Ruble. *Trade Unions in Communist States.* Elmsford, NY: Pergamon Press, 1979.

———. *Soviet Trade Unions.* Cambridge, U.K.: Cambridge University Press, 1981.

Shimada, Haruo. *The Japanese Employment System.* Tokyo: Japanese Institute of Labor, 1980.

Shirai, Taishiro. *Contemporary Industrial Relations in Japan.* Madison: University of Wisconsin Press, 1983.

Sisson, B. Keith. *The Management of Collective Bargaining.* Oxford: Basil Blackwell, 1987.

Stares, Rodney. "The Management of the U.K. Labor Market 1973–1983." Ed. Howard Rosen. *Comparative Labor Market Policies,* Washington: National Council on Employment Policy, 1986.

Streeck, Wolfgang. *Industrial Relations in West Germany.* New York: St. Martin's Press, 1984.

Swedish National Social Insurance Board. *Social Insurance Statistics.* Stockholm: Swedish National Insurance Board, 1987.

Taira, Koji. "Japanese Labor Market Policies." Ed. Howard Rosen. *Comparative Labor Policies,* Washington: National Council on Employment Policy, 1986.

Todd, Graham. *Job Creation in the U.K.* London: Economist Publications, 1986.

Tokunga, Shigeyoshi. "A Marxist Interpretation of Japanese Industrial Relations." Ed. Taishiro Shirai. *Contemporary Industrial Relations in Japan.* Madison: University of Wisconsin Press, 1983.

U.S. Congress, 100th Congress, 1st Session, Joint Economic Committee. *Gorbachev's Economic Plans,* vol. 2. Washington: GPO, November 23, 1987.

U.S. Department of Labor. "The Union of Soviet Socialist Republics." *Foreign Labor Trends.* Washington: GPO, 1989.

U.S. Department of Labor. *Quality of Work Life: AT & T and CWA Examine Process After Three Years.* Washington, GPO, 1985.

U.S. General Accounting Office. *Employee Stock Ownership Plans.* Washington: GPO, February 7, 1986.

INDEX

About the Author

WALTER GALENSON is Jacob Gould Schurman Professor of Economics Emeritus at Cornell University. Since 1949 he has written and published eleven books on the subjects of labor and economics, including: *Labor in Norway*; *The Danish System of Labor Relations*; *The CIO Challenge to the AFL*; *The International Labor Organization: An American View*; *The United Brotherhood of Carpenters and Joiners*; and *A Primer on Employment and Wages*. He has also published some forty articles in various economic, historical, and labor relations journals. He is currently at work on the forthcoming *Economic Growth and Labor Markets in Five Asian Countries*.

DATE DUE

DEMCO NO. 38-298